AF861397

KEYNOTE guide to topics in your course

CLIFFS KEYNOTE REVIEWS

Accounting

by

CLIFFORD M. MASHEB, CPA

Iona College

and

ROBERT B. LEBOWITZ, CPA

Cliff's Notes INCORPORATED

CLIFF'S NOTES, INC. • LINCOLN, NEBRASKA 68501

ISBN 0-8220-1701-6

L.C. Catalogue Card Number: 68-20694

Printed in the United States of America

CONTENTS

TO THE STUDENT

This KEYNOTE is a flexible study aid designed to help you REVIEW YOUR COURSE QUICKLY and USE YOUR TIME TO STUDY ONLY MATERIAL YOU DON'T KNOW.

FOR GENERAL REVIEW

Take the SELF-TEST on the first page of any topic and turn the page to check your answers.

Study the SOLUTIONS to problems and read the EXPLANATIONS of any questions you answered incorrectly.

If you are satisfied with your understanding of the material, move on to another topic.

If you feel that you need further review, read the column of BASIC FACTS and study the column of ILLUSTRATIONS & EXAMPLES.

FOR QUICK REVIEW

Read the column of BASIC FACTS for a rapid review of the essentials of a topic and then take the SELF-TEST if you want to test your understanding of the material.

ADDITIONAL HELP FOR EXAMS

Review terms in the DICTIONARY-INDEX.
Test yourself by taking the sample FINAL EXAMS.

INTRODUCTION: ACCOUNTING—THE LANGUAGE OF BUSINESS

Origin of Accounting. The origin of record-keeping may be traced to the ancient Babylonian civilization. Development of what is considered modern bookkeeping and accounting occurred in Italy during the fourteenth century. The first significant document concerned with double entry bookkeeping was *Summa de Arithmetic Geometrica, Proportioni et Proportionalita* written by Luca Paciali, a Venetian monk, in 1492.

Industrial revolutions in England and America resulted in expanded industry and trade and gave impetus to the evolution of accounting. In the United States, accounting claimed professional status in 1887 with the formation of the American Association of Public Accountants, predecessor to the American Institute of Certified Public Accountants. The development and refinement of accounting theory and practice has greatly accelerated since the early 1930's, due in part to regulations promulgated by the New York and other stock exchanges, formation of the Securities and Exchange Commission, and increasingly complex federal and state tax laws.

Areas of Accounting Activities. Specialized activities requiring the skills of a trained accountant include:

General Accounting and Financial Statement Preparation: the recording, summarizing, and analyzing of business transactions.

Auditing: the independent examination of accounting records and financial statements. This function may be performed by employees of the enterprise (internal auditors) or by Certified Public Accountants (external auditors).

Tax Accounting: the preparation of tax returns and consequences of contemplated income transactions.

Management Services: the assistance given to management in the areas of accounting and finance, including accounting systems installation and analysis.

Cost Accounting and Budgeting: the development and control of product costs and the interpretation of cost data. The budget is a plan or forecast for future financial operations and is used to evaluate actual performance.

Controllership: the chief accounting officer of a company is the controller.

Governmental or Institutional Accounting: the transactions of governmental units, hospitals, colleges and universities, and fraternal and philanthropic organizations.

Accounting Instruction

Role of Accounting in Decision Making. Accounting is concerned with the determination of income and the solvency of the business entity. It provides valuable information needed by management for decision purposes. Data obtained from analysis of the accounting records not only constitutes the past history of the business, but is a guide for future action. The accounting system is informational; it is dynamic in nature rather than static. As society becomes increasingly more complex and the gap between the source of information and the decision maker grows greater, the role of accounting will assume greater importance.

Forms of Business Organization

Individual Proprietorship: A business enterprise owned by a single individual in which almost no preliminary legal requisites exist. The proprietorship equity is represented by a proprietorship account which reflects the net worth of the business (i.e., Marc Richards, Capital).

Partnership: A business enterprise conducted by two or more persons in which a written or oral agreement exists between the parties. The partnership equity is represented by capital accounts detailing each partner's interest.

Corporation: A legal entity given authority to act by a particular state. A charter is granted and the corporation may then issue capital stock and transact business. The stockholder's equity is divided into (1) capital stock, the par or stated value of the amount of the original investment; (2) paid-in-capital, the amount paid in excess of par or stated value; and (3) retained earnings representing the accumulated earnings of the corporation.

The Accounting Equation

Definitions

Assets. These are the economic resources of the business. The items owned include cash, accounts receivable (amounts due from customers), merchandise inventory, land, buildings, investment in stocks and bonds, and intangibles such as patent rights.

Liabilities. These are debts of the business and include accounts payable (amounts due suppliers), notes payable, mortgages payable, and taxes payable.

Capital. This is the claim of the owners against the enterprise.

The Fundamental Accounting Equation. The total of the assets always equals the total of the liabilities and capital. This may be expressed in the following ways:

Assets = Liabilities + Capital
or
Assets – Liabilities = Capital

Balance Sheet. The financial statement entitled the "Balance Sheet" summarizes the assets, liabilities, and capital of the enterprise at a given date. Traditionally, the assets are listed on the left side of the statement in order of their liquidity. Liabilities and capital (Owner's Equity) constitute the right side of the statement. Liabilities appear first, in order of maturity, followed by the capital section.

Income Statement. The Income Statement summarizes the revenue and expenses of an enterprise for a given period of time. A monthly, quarterly, semi-annual, or yearly time period may be involved. The net income or net loss shown is transferred at the end of the accounting period to the capital section of the balance sheet.

Revenue represents the gross increment attributable to business activity. Sources of revenue include sales of merchandise for cash or credit, fees for services rendered and dividend and interest income.

Expenses represent the cost of doing business and are usually related to the production of revenue. Expenses include salaries of employees, cost of merchandise sold, advertising, rent and depreciation.

Marc Richards Company
Balance Sheet
November 30, 19__

Assets		**Liabilities and Owners' Equity**		
		Liabilities		
Cash	$15,000	Accounts payable	$13,000	
Accounts receivable	32,000	Mortgage payable	18,000	
Building	45,000	Total liabilities		$31,000
		Owners' equity:		
		Marc Richards, capital		61,000
	$92,000			$92,000

Marc Richards Company
Income Statement
For the three months ended November 30, 19__

Revenue:		
Commissions earned		$20,000
Expenses:		
Salaries	$8,000	
Rent	2,000	
Advertising	1,000	
Depreciation–building	1,000	12,000
Net Income		$ 8,000

1 RECORDING ACCOUNTING TRANSACTIONS

SELF-TEST

DIRECTIONS: Write your answers (T or F) on the numbered lines to the right. To check your answers, turn to page 5; study the explanations for any questions you missed.

1. The balance sheet is a statement of valuation.
2. The balance sheet presents figures for a period ending or year ending.
3. Net income is determined by subtracting expenses from revenues.
4. Financial statements are prepared at the end of each transaction.
5. A debit to an asset account is a decrease in the account.
6. The total of the debit amounts in a journal entry must equal the credit amounts.
7. The journalizing of transactions occurs after posting to the ledger.
8. "Posting" is the process whereby journal entries are recorded in the ledger.
9. A balanced trial balance will guarantee that no errors exist in the ledger accounts.
10. Taking off a trial balance will facilitate preparation of the financial statements.

ENTER the following transactions in the general journal form. Compare your answers with the correct form given on page 5.

11. R. Smith invested $3,000 cash and $5,000 of inventory in the business.
12. Supplies of $2,000 were purchased on account.
13. Accounts receivable in the amount of $6,000 were collected.
14. R. Smith withdrew $500 for personal use.
15. The accounts payable in question 12 were paid.
16. Office salaries of $150 were paid in cash.

1 ______

2 ______

3 ______

4 ______

5 ______

6 ______

7 ______

8 ______

9 ______

10 ______

BASIC FACTS

The Use of Accounts. The results of the financial transactions for the period are summarized in the *income statement* and the financial position at a given date is reflected in the *balance sheet*. Because of the large number of individual transactions, it is undesirable to prepare financial statements after each transaction. An accounting record has been devised that accumulates the increases and decreases relating to a particular balance sheet or profit and loss item. This is called an **account**. The total of all accounts constitutes a **ledger**. Individual accounts are required for each type of asset, liability, revenue, and expense.

The Double-Entry System—Debit and Credit. In the double-entry system of bookkeeping, at least two accounts are involved in every transaction. Each entry must have an equality of debits and credits. On the conventional balance sheet, the assets are shown on the left side of the statement: therefore, increases in assets are recorded on the left side as debits; decreases on the right side as credits. The credit side of the balance sheet involves liability and owner's equity accounts: therefore, increases are shown as credits; decreases as debits. Since revenue represents an increase in owner's equity, the rules for liability and equity accounts apply. Expenses result in a decrease in equity; therefore, the rules applicable to revenue accounts are reversed.

(*Continued on page 6*)

ILLUSTRATIONS AND EXAMPLES

A Ledger Account

Account Title: Cash — Account #1

Date	Explanation	Ref.	Amount	Date	Explanation	Ref.	Amount
Jan. 1	Investment	CRI	10,000				

In its simplest form the account can be reduced to three elements: (1) the account title identifying the particular item being summarized; (2) a left side, known as the debit side; and (3) a right side, known as the credit side. This can be conveniently reflected in the "T" account.

Account Title	
Debit Side	Credit Side

Cash	
5,000	8,000
4,000	
3,000	

The Double-Entry System—Debit and Credit

Type of Account	Increase	Decrease
Assets	Debit	Credit
Liabilities & Equity	Credit	Debit
Revenues	Credit	Debit
Expenses	Debit	Credit

Recording Transactions in "T" Accounts

Typical transactions for Marc Richards Company are:

1. May 1: Cash of $10,000 is invested by the proprietor.
2. May 3: Furniture and fixtures are purchased for $2,000 in cash.
3. May 7: $6,000 of merchandise is purchased on credit.
4. May 9: Sales on account are made for $10,000.
5. May 15: Office salaries of $250 are paid in cash.
6. May 29: Partial payment of $1,000 is received against sale on account.

Asset—Cash	
(1)10,000	(2) 2,000
(6) 1,000	(5) 250

Asset—Accounts receivable	
(4)10,000	(6) 1,000

Asset—Furniture & fixtures	
(2) 2,000	

Liability—Accounts payable	
	(3) 6,000

Equity—Marc Richards, capital	
	(1)10,000

Revenue—Sales	
	(4)10,000

Expense—Purchases	
(3) 6,000	

Expense—Office salaries	
(5) 250	

(*Continued on page 6*)

EXPLANATIONS

1. *The balance sheet is* not a *statement of valuation.* Most assets are reflected at cost, not current market value.

2. *The balance sheet does* not *present figures for a period ending or a year ending.* The balance sheet is as of a given date.

3. *Net income is determined by subtracting expenses from revenues.*

4. *Financial statements are* not *prepared at the end of each transaction.* They are prepared at the end of an accounting period.

5. *A debit to an asset account is* not a *decrease in the account.* A debit to an asset account is an increase.

6. *The total of the debit amounts in a journal entry must equal the credit amounts.*

7. *The journalizing of transactions* does not *occur after posting to the ledger.* The transactions are first journalized and then posted to the ledger.

8. *"Posting" is the process whereby journal entries are recorded in the ledger.*

9. *A balanced trial balance will* not *guarantee that no errors exist in the ledger accounts.* An omission of a journal entry, a compensating error, or a posting to an incorrect account will go undetected in a balanced trial balance.

10. *Taking off a trial balance will facilitate preparation of the financial statements.*

11.	Cash	3,000	
	Inventory	5,000	
	R. Smith, capital		8,000
12.	Supplies	2,000	
	Accounts payable		2,000
13.	Cash	6,000	
	Accounts receivable		6,000
14.	R. Smith, drawing	500	
	Cash		500
15.	Accounts payable	2,000	
	Cash		2,000
16.	Office salaries expense	150	
	Cash		150

Answer	
F	1
F	2
T	3
F	4
F	5
T	6
F	7
T	8
F	9
T	10

The Journal. Although transactions could be initially recorded from information directly into the ledger accounts, a more efficient method is to use a journal with the ledger. The journal is: (1) the chronological record of all accounting events; and (2) the record of all pertinent information about a transaction.

Posting and the Ledger. Posting is the process whereby the debits and credits of the journal entries are entered in the ledger. After the postings have been completed for the period, account balances may be computed as follows: (1) Add the debits in the particular account and enter the total in small pencil figures just below the last entry in the debit column. (2) Use the same procedure for the credits. (3) Compute the net of the two total figures. If a debit balance results, enter the balancing figure to the left of the last debit entry. If a credit balance results, enter the balancing figure to the left of the last credit entry.

The Trial Balance. After all the accounts have been balanced, it is necessary to establish that an equality of debits and credits exists. This is accomplished by means of "taking off a trial balance." The trial balance is a listing of all the account balances in a ledger, as of a given date. The original transactions have been posted to the "T" accounts; the accounts are now balanced; and a trial balance is prepared.

The trial balance is used for the following purposes: (1) as proof of the equality of the debits and credits, i.e., the ledger is in balance; and (2) as an aid in the preparation of financial statements. It is possible to have a balanced trial balance and still have certain types of errors within the ledger accounts.

Typical of such errors are: (1) The journal entries (debit and/or credit) have been posted to an erroneous account, or accounts. (2) A complete journal entry has been omitted in posting to the ledger. (3) The same entry has been posted more than once. (4) A compensating error has been made, e.g., the debit and credit were both incorrect by an identical amount.

Journal

The previously recorded transactions may now be journalized in the following manner.

Journal

Date		Account Debited	Account Credited	L.F.	Debit	Credit
May	1	Cash			10,000	
			Marc Richards, Capital			10,000
		To record initial investment in the company				
	3	Furniture & fixtures			2,000	
			Cash			2,000
		To record purchase of office equipment for $2,000				
	7	Purchases			6,000	
			Accounts payable			6,000
		Purchase of merchandise from M.R. Sadler & Co.				
	9	Accounts receivable			10,000	
			Sales			10,000
		Sale made to A. Singer for $10,000				
	15	Office salaries			250	
			Cash			250
		Payment of salary for week ending 5/14				
	29	Cash			1,000	
			Accounts receivable			1,000
		Received $1,000 from A. Singer on account				

Posting and the Ledger

An example of how account balances may be computed at the end of an accounting period.

Cash

Oct. 1		18,000	Oct. 3		2,000
2		4,000	5		3,000
8		2,500	6		400
15		1,500			
	20,600	*26,000*			*5,400*

Accounts Payable

Oct. 3		2,000	Oct. 5		15,000
6		3,000	6		5,000
		5,000		*15,000*	*20,000*

Trial Balance

Marc Richards Company

Trial Balance

May 31, 19__

	Debit	Credit
Cash	$ 8,750	
Accounts receivable	9,000	
Furniture & fixtures	2,000	
Accounts payable		$ 6,000
Marc Richards, capital		10,000
Sales		10,000
Purchases	6,000	
Office salaries	250	
	$26,000	$26,000

2 ADJUSTING ENTRIES AND THE WORK SHEET

SELF-TEST

DIRECTIONS: For Questions 1–4, write your answers (a, b, c, or d) on the numbered lines to the right. To check your answers to all questions, turn to page **9**.

1. *The major purpose of closing entries is*
   - a to provide the data to post the ledger to the trial balance
   - b to determine net income
   - c to facilitate the preparation of financial statements
   - d to balance the revenue, expense, and temporary capital accounts so that they may be used to record items for the next period

2. *Salary expense for two days' work in December was accrued. On January 5, the employees were paid $500 for the previous five-day week. The reversing entry is:*
   - a Salaries payable 200
     Salary expense 200
   - b Salary expense 300
     Salaries payable 200
     Cash 500
   - c Salaries payable 500
     Salary expense 500
   - d Salary expense 500
     Cash 500

3. *The item that is* not *an advantage of the work sheet is that it:*
   - a organizes the accounting data
   - b assists in the reconciliation of subsidiary ledgers to control accounts
   - c provides for a classified trial balance
   - d aids in error detection and reduces corrections required in original books of entry

4. *A cash basis accounting system*
   - a is consistent with the matching concept
   - b provides for the proper reporting of cash and non-cash transactions that affect more than one accounting period
   - c reflects entries on the books at the time cash is received or disbursed
   - d records income in the period in which it is earned and charges expenses to the period when incurred

1 ________

2 ________

3 ________

4 ________

A. Smith
Work Sheet For Year Ended June 30, 19__

	Trial Balance		Adjustments		Income Statement		Balance Sheet	
	Dr.	Cr.	Dr.	Cr.	Dr.	Cr.	Dr.	Cr.
Cash	2,300							
Fees receivable	1,600							
Supplies on hand	400							
Prepaid insurance	1,200							
Equipment	2,000							
Accounts payable		2,000						
Wages payable		500						
Smith, capital		3,000						
Fees earned		4,000						
Advertising expense	500							
Wages expense	1,500							
	9,500	9,500						

5. *Record the following adjustments in the Adjustments Column of the work sheet:*
   - a Depreciation of the equipment for the year is $200.
   - b The supplies inventory on June 30 is $250.
   - c Salaries of $300 are to be accrued.
   - d The prepaid insurance of $1,200 represents a three-year policy taken out January 1, 1966.

6. Complete the work sheet.

BASIC FACTS

Cash vs. Accrual Basis Accounting. An accounting system should reflect, as accurately as possible, all of the transactions that have transpired within a given period of time. Many business transactions cannot be started and completed within one accounting period (a month, a year, etc.) The accrual basis of accounting provides for the proper reporting of transactions that affect more than one accounting period.

Accrual Basis Accounting. Income is credited to the period in which it is earned and expenses charged to the period when incurred.

Cash Basis Accounting. Entries are recorded on the books at the time cash is received or disbursed. Transactions of a non-cash nature are generally not recorded, and an accurate picture of income is not presented.

Matching Concept. Accrual accounting is consistent with the concept of matching costs against their related revenues. For example, if a fixed asset has a useful life of twenty years, its cost should be apportioned over this period since benefits will be derived in the form of future revenues.

Adjusting Entries. At the end of an accounting period various kinds of adjusting entries will be required. These entries affect: (1) *unrecorded costs*; (2) *apportionment of recorded costs*; (3) *unrecorded revenues*; and (4) *apportionment of recorded revenues.*

Preparation of the Work Sheet. Before the adjusting and closing entries are recorded in the general journal and posted to the general ledger, a work sheet is prepared.

Advantages of the Use of the Work Sheet. It (1) organizes the accounting data; (2) aids in error detection and reduces corrections required in original books of entry; (3) provides for a classified trial balance; and (4) assists in the preparation of formal financial statements.

Explanation of Work Sheet. The adjustment column reflects the entries discussed under **Adjusting Entries.** The *trial balance* columns taken from the general ledger at the end of the period are combined with the *adjustment* columns to

(*Continued on page 10*)

ILLUSTRATIONS AND EXAMPLES

Adjusting Entries

All adjusting entries refer to the work sheet at the bottom of page **9**.

1. *Unrecorded costs*—Expense items have been incurred but have not been recorded in the journals. This is termed an accrual of an expense.

(Entry #1)	Salary expense	200	
	Salaries payable		200
	To accrue the salary expense for two days' work in December (2/5 × $500).		

2. *Apportionment of Recorded Costs*—Expense items or assets have been recorded in the journals which benefit two or more accounting periods. If an item had been originally expensed, the recording of the unexpended portion (see interest illustration) is termed a deferral of an expense.

(Entry #2)	Prepaid interest	180	
	Interest expense		180
	To record portion of interest expense at December 31, applicable to future accounting periods. December 1 interest for three months totaled $270, recorded as an expense.		
(Entry #3)	Insurance expense	20	
	Prepaid insurance		20
	To record portion of insurance expense at December 31. On December 1, premium of $720 for three-year fire insurance policy was recorded as an asset (1/36 × $720).		
(Entry #4)	Depreciation expense—building	500	
	Accumulated depreciation—building		500
	To record depreciation for month of December. Building cost of $120,000 and an estimated useful life of 20 years (1/12 × 120,000/20).		

3. *Unrecorded Revenues*—Revenues that have been earned but which have not been recorded in journals. This is termed an accrual of income.

(Entry #5)	Commissions receivable	1,500	
	Commission income		1,500
	To record commissions earned on December sales, payment received in January.		

4. *Apportionment of Recorded Revenues*—Income items have been recorded in the journals which will not be earned in the current accounting period. These items are termed deferred credits.

(Entry #6)	Rent income	250	
	Unearned rent		250
	To record liability for January rent received in December and recorded as income.		
(Entry #7)	Unearned interest	400	
	Interest income		400
	To record interest earned at December 31. Interest for two months collected on December 1st, amounting to $800, originally recorded as a liability.		

Note that the use of the words "deferred" and "accrued" do not necessarily have to appear as part of the account title.

(*Continued on page 10*)

Answer

Work Sheet For Year Ended June 30, 19__

	Trial Balance Dr.	Trial Balance Cr.	Adjustments Dr.	Adjustments Cr.	Income Statement Dr.	Income Statement Cr.	Balance Sheet Dr.	Balance Sheet Cr.
Cash	2,300						2,300	
Fees receivable	1,600						1,600	
Supplies on hand	400			(b)150			250	
Prepaid insurance	1,200			(d)200			1,000	
Equipment	2,000						2,000	
Accounts payable		2,000						2,000
Wages payable		500		(c)300				800
Smith, capital		3,000						3,000
Fees earned		4,000				4,000		
Advertising expense	500				500			
Wages expense	1,500		(c)300		1,800			
	9,500	9,500						
Depreciation expense			(a)200		200			
Accumulated depreciation				(a)200				200
Supplies expense			(b)150		150			
Insurance expense			(d)200		200			
			850	850				
					2,850	4,000	7,150	6,000
					1,150			1,150
					4,000	4,000	7,150	7,150

Answer

d	1
a	2
b	3
c	4

RICHARDS REALTY COMPANY
Work Sheet, December 31, 19__

	Trial Balance Dr.	Trial Balance Cr.	Adjustments Dr.	Adjustments Cr.	Adjusted Trial Balance Dr.	Adjusted Trial Balance Cr.	Income Statement Dr.	Income Statement Cr.	Balance Sheet Dr.	Balance Sheet Cr.
Cash	18,420				18,420				18,420	
Rents receivable	1,260				1,260				1,260	
Notes receivable	8,500				8,500				8,500	
Building	120,000				120,000				120,000	
Accumulated depreciation–building		50,000		(4) 500		50,500				50,500
Prepaid insurance	720			(3) 20	700				700	
Accounts payable		7,400				7,400				7,400
Unearned interest		800	(7) 400			400				400
Marc Richards, drawing	10,600				10,600				10,600	
Marc Richards, capital		95,000				95,000				95,000
Rent income		11,300	(6) 250			11,050		11,050		
Commission income		2,250		(5) 1,500		3,750		3,750		
Advertising expense	900				900		900			
Office supplies	820				820		820			
Salary expense	2,600		(1) 200		2,800		2,800			
Interest expense	2,930			(2) 180	2,750		2,750			
Salaries payable				(1) 200		200				200
Prepaid interest			(2) 180		180				180	
Insurance expense			(3) 20		20		20			
Depreciation expense–building			(4) 500		500		500			
Commissions receivable			(5) 1,500		1,500				1,500	
Unearned rent				(6) 250		250				250
Interest income				(7) 400		400		400		
	166,750	166,750	3,050	3,050	168,950	168,950	7,790	15,200	161,160	153,750
							7,410			7,410
							15,200	15,200	161,160	161,160

arrive at the *adjusted trial balance.* Assets, liabilities, and owners' equity accounts are extended to the *balance sheet* columns. Revenues and expense accounts are extended to the *income statement* columns.

All columns are totaled and a balancing figure is inserted in the appropriate income statement column and balance sheet column. If there is a net income for the period, the balancing figure will appear as a debit in the income statement column and a credit in the balance sheet columns. If there is a net loss, the balancing figure will appear as a credit in the income statement and a debit in the balance sheet.

The Closing Entries. At the end of the accounting period revenue, expense, and temporary capital accounts (drawings) are closed.

Reversing Entries. In the following period, certain of the adjusting entries previously recorded require reversal. The reversing entries are dated as of the first day of the new accounting period.

Review of the Accounting Cycle

Record the transaction in the journals.

Post the general ledger and subsidiary ledgers.

Take off a trial balance, usually prepared on the work sheet.

Record adjusting entries on the work sheet.

Complete working papers.

Prepare the financial statements.

Enter adjusting and closing entries in the journal and post the general ledger.

Take a post-closing trial balance.

Closing Entries

Entry I—Transfer of revenue accounts to revenue and expense summary (income summary).

Entry II—Transfer of expense accounts to revenue and expense summary.

Entry III—Transfer revenue and expense summary (net income or loss) to capital account.

Entry IV—Transfer drawing to capital account.

Closing Entries

(1)		
Rent income	11,050	
Commission income	3,750	
Interest income	400	
Revenue and expense summary		15,200
(2)		
Revenue and expense summary	7,790	
Advertising expense		900
Office supplies		820
Salary expense		2,800
Interest expense		2,750
Insurance expense		20
Depreciation—building		500
(3)		
Revenue and expense summary	7,410	
Marc Richards, capital		7,410
(4)		
Marc Richards, capital	10,600	
Marc Richards, drawing		10,600

Reversing Entries

The entry for salaries accrued made on December 31 for $200 must be reversed in January;

Salaries payable	200	
Salary expense		200

If the reversal entry were not made, the expense for January would be overstated by $200 and the liability of $200 would remain on the books.

Salary expense (year 1)

Debit		Credit	
12/31 *adjusting entry #1*	200	12/31 *closed to revenue and expense*	200

Salaries payable (year 1)

Debit		Credit	
1/1 *reversing entry*	200	12/31 *adjusting entry #1*	200

Salary expense (year 2)

Debit		Credit	
1/3	500	1/1 *reversing entry*	200

Cash (year 2)

Debit		Credit	
		1/3	500

3 SPECIALIZED JOURNALS & SUBSIDIARY LEDGERS I

SELF-TEST

DIRECTIONS: Write your answers (a, b, c, or d) on the numbered lines to the right. To check your answers, turn to page **13**.

1. *In posting from the purchase journal, the accountant posted $456 as $546 to the vendor's ledger account. The error would be discovered*
   a when the purchase journal is totaled and balanced
   b when the accounts payable subsidiary ledger is reconciled to the control account
   c when a trial balance is taken for the general ledger and it is out of balance
   d when the certified public accountant audits the transactions for the year

2. *Which type of transaction has been recorded in the wrong journal?*
   a sales of goods on open account–sales journal
   b receipt of cash–cash receipts journal
   c return of merchandise purchased on account–sales returns and allowances journal
   d receipt of note representing an open accounts receivable–general journal

3. *Sales for cash will be recorded in the*
   a sales journal
   b cash receipts journal
   c general journal
   d subsidiary ledger

4. *A single account in the general ledger that summarizes all the account balances in a subsidiary ledger is called a*
   a balance sheet account
   b primary account
   c supporting account
   d control account

5. *In the purchase journal, the total of the invoice is*
   a entered as a credit in the accounts payable column
   b entered as a debit in the accounts payable column
   c entered net of the discount and as a credit in the accounts payable column
   d entered in the sundry column

6. *The subsidiary ledger in which the details of purchases on account are recorded is*
   a the general ledger
   b the accounts receivable ledger
   c the accounts payable ledger
   d none of these

7. *Purchases recorded in the purchase journal for which no separate column is provided are recorded as*
   a debits in the sundry column
   b credits in the sundry column
   c either debits or credits in the sundry column
   d debits in the accounts payable column

8. *Invoices recorded in the purchase journal are posted to the accounts payable subsidiary ledger as*
   a debits
   b credits
   c either debits or credits
   d neither debits, nor credits, since these invoices are recorded in the accounts receivable subsidiary ledger

9. *A "one money column" specialized journal is the*
   a sales journal
   b purchase journal
   c cash receipts journal
   d cash disbursements journal

10. *Specialized journals are used*
   a to accumulate transactions of a similar nature
   b to permit division of labor
   c because of the large number of daily accounting transactions
   d all of these

1 ______
2 ______
3 ______
4 ______
5 ______
6 ______
7 ______
8 ______
9 ______
10 ______

BASIC FACTS

The Multi-Column Specialized Journal. The large number of daily accounting transactions in a business necessitated the development and use of the multi-column specialized journals. These journals provide the means of accumulating transactions of a similar nature and also permit a division of labor.

A journal is called a *book of original entry* because it initially records the transactions which are later entered in the ledger. Most business transactions fall into one of four different categories and, therefore, it is common to find four specialized journals: *sales journal,* for sale of goods on open account; *purchase journal,* for purchase of merchandise on open account; *cash receipts journal,* for receipt of cash; and *cash disbursements journal,* for disbursement of cash.

Sales Journal. When merchandise is sold on credit, the sales are recorded in the sales journal. The accounting document that provides the source for entering this category of transactions is the sales invoice. (The sales journal has columns for entering the important information appearing on the invoice—the date of sale, invoice number, customer's name, and amount of sale.) Each separate sale is entered on a separate line in the sales journal. Each entry gives rise to a debit to accounts receivable and a credit to sales in the same amount. Therefore, only one money column is required. Sales made for cash are not entered in this journal, but are entered in the cash receipts journal.

Subsidiary Ledger—Accounts Receivable. In an actual business situation, the number of sales made during the course of a month may number into the thousands, with hundreds of different customers involved. If each customer's transactions were to be posted to one account called accounts receivable, it would be very difficult to determine at any given date how much was owed by each customer. It is, therefore, necessary that each customer have a separate accounts receivable ledger account maintained in an accounts receivable subsidiary ledger.

In the general ledger the accounts receivable account will reflect the total of all the postings made to the subsidiary accounts receivable ledger from the books of original entry.

Each individual line in the sales journal periodically will be posted as a debit to the appro-

(Continued on page 14)

ILLUSTRATIONS AND EXAMPLES

Sales Journal

Date	Invoice Number	Customer	Post Ref.	Amount
19–				
Sept. 1	414	Roger Allen	√	390
2	415	Robert Byron	√	1,170
14	416	Arthur Clark	√	600
15	417	Jack Davis	√	230
22	418	Clint Evans	√	2,100
29	419	Michael Frank	√	860
				5,350
				(2) (50)

The total of $5,350 is posted to the accounts receivable (Account #2) and to sales (Account #50) in the general ledger.

(Continued on page 14)

EXPLANATIONS

1. *In posting from the purchase journal, the accountant posted $456 as $546 to the vendor's ledger account. The error would be discovered* when the accounts payable subsidiary ledger is reconciled to the control account. This type of error, known as a transposition error, only affects the subsidiary ledger account. When a schedule (trial balance) is taken off of the subsidiary ledger accounts, it will not agree with the control account in the general ledger.

2. *The transaction which has been recorded in the wrong journal is* return of merchandise purchased on account—to sales returns and allowances journal. The sales returns and allowances journal is used to record the return of goods *to* the business. The return of goods purchased *by* the business is entered as a circled figure in the purchase journal, or in a special purchase returns and allowances journal.

3. *Sales for cash will be recorded in the* cash receipts journal, as are all items involving the receipt of cash. A sale for cash is reflected in this book of original entry with a credit to the sales account. The sales journal is utilized only to record sales on open account.

4. *A single account in the general ledger that summarizes all the account balances in a subsidiary ledger is called* a control account. The control account in the general ledger is used to take the place of numerous individual accounts.

5. *In the purchase journal, the total of the invoice is* entered as a credit in the accounts payable column. This is the total liability due to the supplier.

6. *The subsidiary ledger in which the details of purchases on account are recorded is* the accounts payable ledger. The general ledger is not a subsidiary ledger; the accounts receivable ledger records details of sales of goods or services made on open account.

7. *Purchases recorded in the purchase journal for which no separate column is provided are recorded as* debits in the sundry column, which is used as a catchall to record items which are not repetitive in nature and, therefore, do not require a separate column. The expense portion of purchase journal transactions is recorded as debits.

8. *Invoices recorded in the purchase journal are posted to the accounts payable subsidiary ledger as* credits. Transactions in the subsidiary ledger must be identical with the treatment given in the general ledger control account. The liability in the general ledger is entered as a credit to accounts payable. The individual postings to the subsidiary ledger, therefore, must also be credits.

9. *A "one money column" specialized journal is the* sales journal. It is a specialized journal which records only one type of transaction, a sale on open account. Every entry requires a debit to accounts receivable and a credit to sales of an equal amount. It is possible to use only one money column, posting the total as a debit to the accounts receivable control account and as a credit to the sales account in the general ledger.

10. *Specialized journals are used* to accumulate transactions of a similar nature, to permit division of labor, and because of the large number of daily accounting transactions. The most common specialized journals are cash receipts, cash disbursements, purchase, and sales.

Answer	
b	**1**
c	**2**
b	**3**
d	**4**
a	**5**
c	**6**
a	**7**
b	**8**
a	**9**
d	**10**

priate account in the subsidiary ledger. A check mark is made in the posting reference column to indicate that the posting has been made.

At the end of each accounting period, the total of the balances in the individual accounts of the subsidiary ledger must be in agreement with the balance in the general ledger accounts receivable control.

Purchase Journal. The purchase journal is used to record transactions with the suppliers of goods and services to the business enterprise. The purchase invoice is the accounting document that provides the source for entry in this journal. The total of the invoice is entered as a credit to the accounts payable column. Provision is made in the journal for separate columns to accumulate debits to frequently used accounts, such as merchandise purchases, store supplies, and office expenses. In addition, a sundry column is used for entering debits to other accounts.

At the end of the month, the individual columns are totaled and posted to the general ledger. The sundry column is not entered in total, but posted to the individual general ledger accounts involved. The total of the debit columns must be in agreement with the accounts payable credit column.

Subsidiary Ledger—Accounts Payable. Each account is credited periodically in the accounts payable subsidiary ledger. At the time of posting, a check mark is entered in the posting reference column. At the end of the accounting period, the balance in the individual creditor accounts are totaled and must be in agreement with the accounts payable control in the general ledger.

Purchase Journal

Date	Account Credited	Post Ref.	Accounts Payable Cr.	Merchandise Purchases Dr.	Store Supplies Dr.	Office Expense Dr.	Sundry Accounts Dr.		
							Account	Post. Ref.	Amount
Sept. 5	E&C Company	√	500			500			
12	Queens Inc.	√	2,500				Furniture	12	2,500
17	Flushing Supplies Co.	√	800		800				
20	Black Manufacturing Co.	√	5,745	5,745					
23	Towers Ins. Co.	√	625				Prepaid insurance	18	625
25	Martin Mfg.	√	3,250	3,250					
			13,420	8,995	800	500			3,125
			(30)	(60)	(61)	(62)			(√)

4 SPECIALIZED JOURNALS & SUBSIDIARY LEDGERS II

SELF-TEST

The following accounts appear in the general ledger of the D. Greene Co. as of March 1:

101	Cash	$ 8,500	200 D. Greene, capital	37,825
110	Accounts receivable	4,800	201 D. Greene, drawing	
115	Merchandise inventory	15,000	500 Sales	
116	Store supplies	425	501 Sales returns and allowances	
117	Prepaid insurance	600	502 Sales discounts	
120	Equipment	18,000	600 Purchases	
121	Accumulated depreciation	3,000	601 Purchases discounts	
150	Accounts payable	6,500	701 Advertising expense	
			801 Rent expense	

The details of the subsidiary ledgers are presented below:

Accounts Receivable

Robert Adams	$1,000
L & M Corp.	1,500
Max Post	800
Research Inc.	1,250
Steiner Co.	250
	$4,800

Accounts Payable

New Rochelle Supply Co.	$3,000
Jones Co.	1,500
B. Miller Co.	2,000
	$6,500

Required:

1. Record the following transactions for March, using the appropriate journals. To check your answer, turn to page 17.

March	2	Purchase supplies on account from New Rochelle Supply Co.	$ 800
	2	Merchandise sold to Steiner Co. was returned.	250
	3	Check No. 810 issued to Jones Co. in payment of invoice for $1,500, less 2% discount.	
	5	Sold merchandise on account to L & M Corp. Invoice No. 301.	825
	6	Purchased merchandise on account from Jones Co.	1,200
	8	Received check from Robert Adams in payment of invoice for $1,000, less 2% discount.	
	9	Check No. 811 issued for payment of March rent.	750
	10	Purchased equipment on account from Marks Mfg.	1,000
	10	Received check from L & M Corp. in payment of invoice $1,500, less 2% discount.	
	12	Cash sale to S & S Inc. for $1,200, less 2% discount.	
	12	Sold merchandise on account to Robert Adams, invoice No. 302.	1,400
	15	Sold merchandise on account to Steiner Co., invoice No. 303.	600
	18	Purchased merchandise on account from Jones Co.	1,500
	18	Issued check No. 812 for cash purchases from B.S.S. Ltd. for $1,050, no discount.	
	20	Sold merchandise on account to Max Post, invoice No. 304.	550
	25	Issued check No. 813 for advertising expenses to the New York Times.	25
	25	Received check from Max Post in payment of invoice $800, no discount.	

2. Post the entries in the journals to "T" accounts representing the general ledger and subsidiary ledger accounts. To check your answers, turn to page 18.

BASIC FACTS

Cash Receipts Journal. All transactions involving cash receipts are entered in the cash receipts journal. Special columns are provided for items of a repetitive nature. The debit columns, in addition to the cash column, will usually include a sales discounts column. The credit columns, in addition to accounts receivable, will include a sales column and a sundry accounts column. At the end of the month, the journal must be totaled, agreement between the debits and credits must be determined, and postings made to the general ledger accounts. At more frequent intervals, the individual postings to the accounts receivable subsidiary ledger must be made.

Cash Disbursements Journal. The cash disbursements or cash payments journal records all cash transactions made by check. As in the cash receipts journal, special columns are provided to handle items that occur frequently. End-of-month procedures are similar to those employed in the cash receipts journal. At regular intervals, payments affecting accounts payable are posted to the individual subsidiary accounts.

General Journal. Any transactions which cannot be recorded in the specialized journals must be entered in a general journal. Where an item affects a "control" account (accounts receivable or accounts payable), a posting must be made to the general ledger account as well as to the individual subsidiary ledger account. An explanation of the entry must appear in the journal.

Other Journals. In various situations, it may be practicable to record transactions in specialized journals rather than the general journal. Examples will include notes receivable, sales returns and allowances, purchase returns and allowances, and petty cash journal.

Summary Posting From Journals. In the general ledger and subsidiary ledgers, indication is made of the journal which provided the source of the entry.

ILLUSTRATIONS AND EXAMPLES

GENERAL JOURNAL

19__		L.F.		
Sept. 26	Notes receivable	3	390	
	Accounts receivable (Roger Allen) . . .	(2)(√)		390
	Received 60 day non-interest bearing note for purchase of September 1.			

CASH RECEIPTS JOURNAL

		DEBITS					CREDITS				
				Sundry				Accounts Receivable			
Date	Explanation	Cash	Sales Discounts	Account	L.F.	Amount	Account Credited	L.F.		Sales	Sundry Amount
19__ Sept. 2	Cash sales	400								400	
4	Invoice July 27, less 2%	784	16				Robert Byron	√	800		
5	Invoice August 29, less 2%	2,352	48				Jack Davis	√	2,400		
6	Collection of notes receivable	1,500					Notes receivable	14			1,500
12	Cash sales	640								640	
14	Invoice August 15, less 2%	3,528	72				Michael Frank	√	3,600		
15	Obtained 60 day bank loan	15,000					Notes payable	35			15,000
18	Invoice August 20, less allowance and 2% discount	2,646	54	Sales returns and Allowances	52	100	Roger Allen	√	2,800		
22	Cash sales	380								380	
		27,230	190			100			9,600	1,420	16,500
		(1)	(53)						(2)	(50)	

CASH DISBURSEMENTS

			CREDITS					DEBITS				
					Sundry				Accounts Payable			Sundry
Date	Check No.	Explanation	Cash	Purchase Discounts	Name	L.F.	Amount	Accounts Debited	L.F.	Amount	Purchases	Amount
19__ Sept. 2	404	Invoice of Aug. 25, less 2%	686	14				Martin Mfg.	√	700		
7	405	Purchased typewriter	285					Office Equipment	15			285
8	406	Invoice of July 15	350					E & C Company	√	350		
9	407	Paid Sept. rent	450					Rent	80			450
10	408	Cash purchase	130								130	
15	409	Paid note with 6% interest for 4 months	2,550					Notes payable	35			2,500
								Interest expense	92			50
			4,451	14						1,050	130	3,285
			(1)	(65)						(30)	(60)	

Answers

SALES JOURNAL

Date	Invoice Number	Customer	L.F.	Amount
19__				
March 5	301	L & M Corp.	√	825
12	302	Robert Adams	√	1,400
15	303	Steiner Co.	√	600
20	304	Max Post	√	550
				3,375
				(110) (500)

PURCHASE JOURNAL

Date	Account Credited	L.F.	Accounts Payable (Cr.)	Purchases (Dr.)	Store Supplies (Dr.)	Sundry Accounts: Account	Sundry Accounts: L.F.	Amount (Dr.)
March 2	New Rochelle Supply Co.	√	800		800			
6	Jones Co.	√	1,200	1,200				
10	Marks Mfg.	√	1,000			Equipment	120	1,000
18	Jones Co.	√	1,500	1,500				
			4,500	2,700	800			1,000
			(150)	(600)	(116)			(√)

CASH DISBURSEMENTS JOURNAL

Date	Check no.	Explanation	CREDITS: Cash	CREDITS: Purchase Discounts	DEBITS: Accounts Debited	Accounts Payable: L.F.	Accounts Payable: Amount	Purchases	Sundry: L.F.	Sundry: Amounts
March 3	810	Invoice of 2/25, less 2%	1,470	30	Jones Co.	√	1,500			
9	811	Paid March rent	750		Rent				801	750
18	812	Cash purchase, B.S.S. Ltd.	1,050					1,050		
25	813	N.Y. Times, advertising	25		Advertising				701	25
			3,295	30			1,500	1,050		775
			(101)	(601)			(150)	(600)		(√)

GENERAL JOURNAL

Date		L.F.		
March 2	Sales returns and allowances.	501	250	
	Accounts receivable–Steiner Co. . .	110/√		250

CASH RECEIPTS JOURNAL

Date	Account Credited	L.F.	Cash (Dr.)	Sales Discounts (Dr.)	Sales (Cr.)	Accounts Receivable (Cr.)
19__						
March 8	Robert Adams	√	980	20		1,000
10	L. M. Corp.	√	1,470	30		1,500
12	S & S Inc.		1,176	24	1,200	
25	Max Post	√	800			800
			4,426	74	1,200	3,300
			(101)	(502)	(500)	(110)

(Answers continued on page 18)

General Ledger:

101 Cash

3/1		8,500	3/31	CD	3,295
3/31	CR	4,426			

110 Accounts Receivable

3/1		4,800	3/31	CR	3,300
3/31	SJ	3,375	3/2	GJ	250

115 Merchandise Inventory

3/1		15,000			

116 Store Supplies

3/1		425			
3/31	PJ	800			

117 Prepaid Insurance

3/1		600			

120 Equipment

3/1		18,000			
3/10	PJ	1,000			

121 Accumulated Depreciation

			3/1		3,000

150 Accounts Payable

3/31	CD	1,500	3/1		6,500
			3/31	PJ	4,500

200 D. Greene, Capital

			3/1		37,825

201 D. Greene, Drawing

500 Sales

			3/31	SJ	3,375
			3/31	CR	1,200

501 Sales Returns & Allowances

3/2	GJ	250			

502 Sales Discounts

3/31	CR	74			

600 Purchases

3/31	PJ	2,700			
3/31	CD	1,050			

601 Purchases Discounts

			3/31	CD	30

701 Advertising Expense

3/25	CD	25			

801 Rent Expense

3/9	CD	750			

Accounts Receivable:

Robert Adams

3/1		1,000	3/8	CR	1,000
3/12	SJ	1,400			

L & M Corp.

3/1		1,500	3/10	CR	1,500
3/5	SJ	825			

Max Post

3/1		800	3/25	CR	800
3/20	SJ	550			

Research Inc.

3/1		1,250			

Steiner Co.

3/1		250	3/2	GJ	250
3/15	SJ	600			

Accounts Payable:

New Rochelle Supply Co.

			3/1		3,000
			3/2	PJ	800

Jones Co.

3/3	CD	1,500	3/1		1,500
			3/6	PJ	1,200
			3/18	PJ	1,500

B. Miller Co.

			3/1		2,000

Marks Mfg.

			3/10	PJ	1,000

5 PREPARATION OF FINANCIAL STATEMENTS & MERCHANDISE OPERATIONS

SELF-TEST

The categories listed in the right column appear on the balance sheet and income statement of a merchandising company. Classify each of the following accounts by writing your answer, a–k, on the numbered lines to the right. To check your answers, turn to page 21.

Accounts	Categories	Answers
1. *Allowance for bad debts*	a Current assets	1 ____
2. *Land held for investment*	b Fixed assets (plant and equipment)	2 ____
3. *Interest income*	c Other assets	3 ____
4. *Bad debts expense*	d Current liabilities	4 ____
5. *Merchandise inventory–Beginning of period*	e Long-term liabilities	5 ____
6. *Sales returns and allowances*	f Owners' equity	6 ____
7. *Bonds payable*	g Sales	7 ____
8. *Freight-in*	h Cost of goods sold	8 ____
9. *Proprietor's drawing account*	i Selling, general, and administrative expenses	9 ____
10. *Furniture and fixtures*	j Other income	10 ____
11. *Marketable securities*	k Other expenses	11 ____
12. *Current maturities of long-term debt*		12 ____
13. *Leasehold improvements*		13 ____
14. *Interest expense*		14 ____
15. *Purchase discounts*		15 ____

BASIC FACTS

Types of Statements. The two fundamental financial statements are the *balance sheet*, a statement of position as of a given date, and the *income statement*, a statement reflecting the operation for a given period of time. A third statement, being used with increasing frequency, is the *funds statement* (See Chapter 21).

Form of the Balance Sheet. The information appearing on a simplified balance sheet is usually classified as follows:

Current Assets are assets which are expected to be realized in cash or consumed in the normal operating cycle of the business. Included are cash, notes and accounts receivable, marketable securities, inventories, and prepaid items.

Fixed Assets are assets with a useful life extending beyond the current business year. They are intended for use in the operations of the business and are not held for sale. Items included are land, buildings, equipment, furniture, and intangibles such as patents, leasehold improvements, and goodwill. The accumulated depreciation and amortization is deducted from the applicable fixed asset account.

Other Assets are those that cannot be classified as either current or fixed and include such items as long-term receivables, deferred charges, and land held for investment purposes.

Current Liabilities are liabilities that will require the use of current assets or the creation of other current liabilities for their liquidation. They must be paid within the current operating cycle or one year, whichever is longer. Included are accounts and notes payable, current maturities of long-term debt, taxes, and expenses payable.

The current asset and current liability categories are used as measures of the liquidity of a business, i.e., its potential ability to meet obligations. The ratio of current assets to current liabilities is known as the *current ratio*. The ratio of *working capital* (excess of current assets over current liabilities) to current liabilities is another measure of financial strength.

(*Continued on page 22*)

ILLUSTRATIONS AND EXAMPLES

Marc Richards Company

Balance Sheet

December 31, 19__

Assets

Current assets			
Cash		$15,400	
Marketable securities		7,400	
Accounts receivable	$49,000		
Less allowance for doubtful accounts	2,290	46,710	
Merchandise inventory		32,500	
Prepaid expenses		430	
Total current assets			$102,440
Property			
Building	80,000		
Less accumulated depreciation	49,000	31,000	
Furniture and equipment	8,600		
Less accumulated depreciation	3,950	4,650	
Total property			35,650
Other assets			
Deferred financing charges			2,350
Total assets			$140,440

Liabilities and Owner's Equity

Current liabilities			
Notes payable		$11,675	
Accounts payable		39,750	
First mortgage 4% bonds due current year		13,000	
Federal income tax payable		7,950	
Accrued expenses		6,800	
Total current liabilities			$ 79,175
Long-term debt			
Mortgage payable		38,700	
Less current maturities		13,000	
Total long-term debt			25,700
Total liabilities			104,875
Owner's equity			
Marc Richards, capital, January 1, 19__		25,900	
Net income for the year	$24,665		
Less proprietor's drawing	15,000		
Increase in capital		9,665	
Marc Richards, capital, December 31, 19__			35,565
Total liabilities and owner's equity			$140,440

(*Continued on page 22*)

EXPLANATIONS

1. *Allowance for bad debts is classified as* current assets. This account is an asset valuation which appears as a deduction from the asset account, accounts receivable. Since accounts receivable is a current asset, the asset valuation account is also classified as a current asset.

2. *Land held for investment is classified as* other assets. Since the land is not used in the operation of the business, it should not be classified as a fixed asset.

3. *Interest income is classified as* other income since it is not directly related to business operations.

4. *Bad debts expense is classified as* selling, general, and administrative expense. The preferred treatment is to include bad debts in general expenses since bad debt losses are a normal cost of doing business.

5. *Merchandise inventory–beginning of period is classified as* cost of goods sold. This is the initial item appearing in the cost of goods sold category, to which is added purchases and freight costs. From this total the ending inventory is subtracted to arrive at the cost of sales.

6. *Sales returns and allowances are classified as* sales. Sales returns and allowances appear as a deduction from the sales figure.

7. *Bonds payable are classified as* long-term liabilities. Debts whose maturity is more than one year from the balance sheet date are classified as long-term liabilities. Bonds payable would be classified as "long term" except for that portion which falls due within the year.

8. *Freight-in is classified as* cost of goods sold. Freight-in is considered as an additional cost of acquiring merchandise and, like merchandise purchases, appears in the cost of goods sold section.

9. *Proprietor's drawing account is classified as* owners' equity. This item reduces owners' equity.

10. *Furniture and fixtures are classified as* fixed assets. Furniture and fixtures are property utilized in the operations of the business.

11. *Marketable securities are classified as* current assets. However, securities held for purposes of control or other long-term investment purposes are classified as "investments," rather than current assets.

12. *Current maturities of long-term debt are classified as* current liabilities. Any liability whose liquidation can reasonably be expected to require the use of current assets should be treated as a current liability. Current maturities of long-term debt come within this definition.

13. *Leasehold improvements are classified as fixed assets.* This account incorporates the cost incurred in improvements made to leased property. It represents items that become part of rented real property (e.g., cost of electrical wiring to leased premises) having a life of more than one year.

14. *Interest expense is classified as* other expense. Normally, this item is treated as an other expense item, since the expense is financial in nature rather than being directly related to the operations of the business (selling, general, and administrative expense).

15. *Purchase discounts are classified as* cost of goods sold because they are usually reflected as a reduction of the merchandise purchases. Some accountants choose to show both sales and purchase discounts below net income from operations in the other expense and other income categories respectively.

Answers

a	1
c	2
j	3
i	4
h	5
g	6
e	7
h	8
f	9
b	10
a	11
d	12
b	13
k	14
h	15

Long-term Liabilities are liabilities that do not satisfy the requirements for current liabilities. They include such items as mortgages payable and bonds payable.

The Owner's Equity section appears differently in a corporate balance sheet than it does in one for a single proprietorship. A corporate statement reflects the separate elements of capital stock and of retained earnings. The balance sheet for a proprietorship has a single owners' equity account.

Income Statement. A *multiple-step* income statement is normally prepared for a merchandising operation. A *single-step* statement, in which all expenses and costs are deducted as a single figure from the total income, has less general use. The multiple-step merchandising income statement includes the following sections:

Sales is the gross charge for merchandise, reduced by returns, allowances, and discounts.

Cost of Goods Sold includes the beginning inventory plus net purchases for the period, less inventory at the end of the period. The purchases item includes gross purchases less purchase returns, allowances, and discounts (trade and cash), plus freight and transportation charges.

Gross Profit on Sales is the excess of net sales over the cost of goods sold. Some statements refer to this item as gross margin.

Selling, General, and Administrative Expenses are expenses incurred directly by the normal merchandising operations of the business. There is much latitude in the classification of these expenses, but it is not unusual to find the two categories of *selling* and *general* expenses in use.

Net Income (or Loss) from Operations is the balance remaining after subtracting selling, general, and administrative expenses from the gross profit on sales.

Other Income and Expenses include items of a non-operating nature. In a merchandising operation, income from the sale of fixed assets and from dividends are examples of other income. Interest expenses would be considered an other expense item.

Net Income (or Loss) is the net income (or loss) from operations, adjusted for non-operating income and expense items.

Marc Richards Company

Statement of Income

For the Year Ending December 31, 19__

Sales			$450,000
Cost of goods sold			
Merchandise inventory, January 1, 19__		$ 28,600	
Purchases, net		284,950	
Freight in		3,450	
Cost of goods available for sale		317,000	
Merchandise inventory, December 31, 19__		32,000	
Cost of goods sold			285,000
Gross profit on sales			$165,000
Operating expenses			
Selling expenses			
Salaries–sales	$29,500		
Advertising	24,500		
Promotion	15,545		
Total selling expenses		$ 69,545	
General expenses			
Salaries–administration	$38,000		
Rent	12,000		
Telephone and telegraph	8,500		
Professional fees	6,000		
Depreciation–building	2,400		
Depreciation–furniture and equipment	860		
Insurance	1,220		
Total general expenses		$ 68,980	
Total operating expenses			138,525
Total income from operations			$ 26,475
Interest expense on mortgage bonds			1,810
Net income			$ 24,665

6 CASH, PETTY CASH, & INVESTMENTS

SELF-TEST

1. Prepare a bank reconciliation for A & B Company on December 31, based on the following information:

Checkbook balance, December 31		$5,511
Deposit in transit		250
Outstanding checks:		
Check #578	$200	
Check #582	86	
Check #583	142	
NSF check of F. Smith		212
Note receivable, collected by bank		1,000
December bank charges		2
Bank charged a check of the AB Vending Co., in error		55
Bank statement balance, December 31		6,420

2. Give the journal entries in general journal form for the following transactions:

February 1, 1968	Purchased $10,000 par value 6% bonds of Bendix Co. at 102 and accrued interest. Interest dates are January 1 and July 1. The bonds mature on January 1, 1978.
July 1	Received the semi-annual interest on the Bendix Co. bonds.
December 31	Accrue interest earned to the end of the year and amortize the bond premium for the eleven months.

To CHECK your answers, turn to page 25.

BASIC FACTS

Composition of Cash and Cash on Hand. Cash includes any medium of exchange that can be deposited in a bank for immediate credit to the depositor's account, such as checks, money orders, and demand and time deposits. IOU's and postage stamps are not considered cash.

Internal Control is that part of the system which relates to the plans and procedures established to: (1) safeguard the company's assets; (2) achieve accurate accounting data; (3) encourage efficient operation; and (4) measure adherence to corporate policies.

Internal Control Applied to Cash Receipts. (1) Cash receipts should be deposited intact daily. (2) Incoming mail should be opened by a responsible employee other than the cashier or bookkeeper. Cash items received should be entered on a list prepared in duplicate. (3) The employee handling cash sales should have no access to the cash receipts journal or to the ledgers. (4) Deposit slips should be prepared in duplicate. (5) Cash sales should be recorded on pre-numbered sales invoices. (6) If practicable, a cash register should be used to ring up every cash sale in view of the customer.

Internal Control Applied to Cash Disbursements. (1) In general, all disbursements should be made by check. (2) Checks should be accounted for by having them pre-numbered. (3) Documents supporting the payment should be cancelled at the time the check is signed. (4) The person who signs the check should not also authorize payment of the invoice. (5) An independent reconciliation of the bank accounts and the general ledger balance should be prepared monthly.

Reconciling the Bank Account. At the end of any given month, the book balance in the cash accounts will not be in agreement with the monthly bank statement. These differences are due to a time lag by either the company or the bank, in recording transactions and errors.

Bank Reconciliation Procedures. (1) The bank deposits, as shown on the bank statement, should be compared with the deposits as entered in the cash receipts journal. Deposits made near the end of

(Continued on page 25)

ILLUSTRATIONS AND EXAMPLES

Typical Reconciling Items

Adjustments to the Bank's Balance

Additions: *Deposits in transit* representing items recorded in the company's cash receipts journal but as yet not recorded by the bank.

Deductions: Outstanding checks representing checks issued and recorded by the company but not clearing the bank by the statement date.

Adjustments to the Book's Balance

Additions: *Notes receivable* collected by the bank but not recorded on the books.

Deductions: (1) *Service charge* not recorded by the company; (2) *NSF (not sufficient funds) checks* returned by the bank; (3) *Notes payable* of the company paid by the bank for our account.

Errors made by either the bank or the company would be shown on the reconciliation.

Illustrative Bank Reconciliation

MARC RICHARDS COMPANY
Bank Reconciliation In Account With
State Bank and Trust Company
September 30, 19__

Book balance, September 30, 19__			$6,432.19
Add: Note receivable collected by bank			1,325.00
			$7,757.19
Deduct: NSF check of G. Grand		$147.50	
September bank charge		5.50	
Error in recording Ck. #802		45.00	198.00
Adjusted balance, September 30, 19__			$7,559.19
Bank balance, September 30, 19__			$8,741.20
Add: Deposit of September 30, 19__, in transit			437.50
			$9,178.70
Deduct: Outstanding checks			
	#817	$632.29	
	#843	98.22	
	#844	216.83	
	#845	672.17	1,619.51
Adjusted balance, September 30, 19__			$7,559.19

The Petty Cash Fund

Creation of the Fund. The fund is established by recording the following entry:

Petty Cash	50.00	
Cash		50.00

Disbursements. At the time of disbursement, a voucher indicating the amount of payment is prepared and signed by the recipient. No entry in the books of the company is required.

(Continued on page 26)

ANSWERS

1.

A & B Company
Bank Reconciliation
December 31, 19––

Book balance, December 31, 19––		$5,511
Add: Note receivable, collected by bank		1,000
		6,511
Deduct: NSF check of F. Smith	$212	
December bank charges	2	214
Adjusted balance, December 31, 19__		$6,297
Bank balance, December 31, 19––		$6,420
Add: Deposit in transit	$250	
Bank error in charging a check of the AB Vending Co	55	305
		$6,725
Deduct: outstanding checks:		
#578	$200	
#582	86	
#583	142	428
Adjusted balance, December 31, 19__		$6,297

2.

February 1	Investment in Bendix Co. bonds	10,200	
	Bond interest receivable ($10,000 x 6% x 1/12)	50	
	Cash		10,250
July 1	Cash ($10,000 x 3%)	300	
	Bond interest receivable		50
	Interest income		250
Dec. 31	Bond interest receivable	300	
	Interest income		300
	Bond interest income	18.49	
	Investment in Bendix Co. bonds. ($200 x 11/119)		18.49

(*Basic Facts continued*)
the month and not reflected on the bank statement presumably are deposits in transit. (2) The returned checks should be placed in numerical order and compared with the entries made in the cash disbursements journal. Checks not clearing are considered to be outstanding checks. (3) Bank debit and credit memoranda should be checked against the cash journals to ascertain if they have been recorded. (4) Any errors that are recorded require recognition on the bank reconciliation.

The Petty Cash Fund. Petty disbursements, i.e., under $25.00, are usually handled through a petty cash fund which is reimbursed periodically by check. The fund is usually maintained on an *imprest basis*, which requires that the total of the cash and vouchers equal the amount of the account balance in the general ledger.

(*Continued on page 26*)

Investments. The most common investments include stocks or bonds of a domestic corporation, U. S. government securities, municipal bonds, mortgages, and long-term notes.

Classification on the Balance Sheet. Investments are classified as either current assets, or long-term investments.

If treated as *current assets,* they must be readily marketable and there must be an intention on the part of management to convert the investments to satisfy the cash demands of the normal operating cycle. The usual balance sheet terminology for these assets is *marketable securities* and they appear on the balance sheet immediately after cash.

The total security holding, rather than each individual security, is valued at cost, or at the lower of cost or market. The method of valuation is shown parenthetically or by footnote.

Long-term Investments are not intended to meet the cash needs of the business and are permanent in nature. The securities are valued at cost unless there has been a substantial permanent decline in value, in which case the cost is appropriately reduced.

Recording the Investment. The cost includes the price paid plus commissions and taxes. In the case of common stocks, dividends are usually paid quarterly and do not accrue daily. When bonds are purchased, the accrued interest to date is recorded on the purchaser's books.

Recording Income from Investments. (1) *Stocks*: Cash dividends may be recorded at the time of declaration or receipt. A stock dividend (paid in the form of additional shares of the security, instead of cash) does not require a journal entry. Each original share of stock now has a reduced cost basis computed by dividing the original cost price by the total number of shares held. (2) *Bonds*: At the end of the accounting period the accrued interest is recorded to date. If the bonds are considered current assets, the fact that they were purchased at a premium or discount is ignored for purposes of amortization. In certain instances, e.g. large institutional investors, adjustments to the bond interest income account are made for the premium or discount on permanent bond investments.

Replenishment of the Fund. When the cash in the fund goes below an established minimum requirement, a reimbursement check is drawn for the amount of the previously paid vouchers. At this time, the disbursements from the fund are entered on the books of the company. A typical entry would be:

Office supplies	9.40	
Car fares	2.15	
Employee advance	10.00	
Postage	20.00	
Cash		41.55

Investments

Recording The Investment

Investment in bonds	10,262.50	
Bond interest receivable (or interest income)	100.00	
Cash		10,362,50

Acquisition of $10,000 4% bond in XYZ Corporation, due in 10 years, purchased at 102 ($1,020 for each $1,000 bond) plus accrued interest from March 1, 19-- to May 31, 19--. Commissions were $62.50.

Recording Income From Investments

Stocks. If recorded at the time of declaration, the following entry would be made:

Dividends receivable
Dividends income

Bonds.

Bond interest receivable	16.66	
Bond interest income		16.66

To record 4% interest on $5,000 bond for month of December.

In the first illustration of recording the bonds, the premium paid, including commissions, was $262.50. For a one-year period, the entry to record the amortization is as follows:

Bond interest income	26.25	
Investment in bonds		26.25

To record 1/10 of $262.50 as amortization.

Gains and Loss From Security Transactions. The journal entries to record the sale of a security are identical for temporary and permanent investments.

Stocks

Cash	1,735	
Loss on sale of securities	265	
Marketable securities		2,000

Sold 100 shares XYZ Corporation stock @$18., less brokerage commission of $65. Securities purchased at $20 per share.

Bonds

Interest receivable	15	
Interest income		15

To record interest income accrued to date of sale.

Cash	1,180	
Interest receivable		15
Investment in bonds		1,000
Gain on sale of bonds		165

To record sale of $1,000 bond (purchased at par) @ 120, plus accrued interest. Commissions totaled $35.

7 ACCOUNTS RECEIVABLE & NOTES RECEIVABLE

SELF-TEST

DIRECTIONS: For questions 1–10, write your answers (T or F) on the numbered lines to the right. To check your answers to all questions, turn to page 29.

1. Receivables that are expected to be realized in more than one year are normally classified as current assets.

2. Bad debts losses should be accounted for before an actual loss has taken place.

3. The direct charge-off method of recognizing future credit losses follows the accounting concept that expenses should be matched against the related revenue.

4. The allowance for doubtful accounts normally has a *debit* balance.

5. On the balance sheet the allowance for doubtful accounts is subtracted from accounts receivable.

6. The purpose of aging accounts receivable is to estimate the probable bad debt expense.

7. In the aging of accounts receivable, the percentage uncollectible increases with the length of time the account is past due.

8. The percentage of net sales as a determination of the probable bad debt expense is considered the most sophisticated method.

9. Under the direct charge-off method the account to be credited for a bad debt recovery is bad debt expense.

10. Bad debt expense is shown on the income statement as a deduction from gross sales.

11. Give the journal entries in general journal form for the following transactions:

June 6 Sold merchandise to Philip Jones in amount of $3,000.
July 7 Received Philip Jones' 60 day 6% interest-bearing note for $1,880, dated July 7, and cash in amount of $1,120.
July 17 Discounted this note at 6% at National Bank.
Sept. 6 Bank notified us that Philip Jones dishonored his note at maturity, and that our account has been charged for the note and protest fees amounting to $2.50.

1 ______
2 ______
3 ______
4 ______
5 ______
6 ______
7 ______
8 ______
9 ______
10 ______

BASIC FACTS

Classification on the Balance Sheet. Trade accounts and notes receivable represent monies due from credit sales transactions. Other receivables include loans to employees and advances to affiliated companies. These items are recorded in the general ledger in separate accounts and are usually segregated from trade receivables when presented on the balance sheet.

Only receivables expected to be realized in cash within one year are classified as *current assets*; long-term receivables appear below current assets in a classification such as *investments* or *other assets.*

Valuation of Accounts Receivable. At the end of any accounting period, recognition must be given to those receivables that will never be fully realized. There are two methods for recognizing these future credit losses:

(1) Direct Charge-Off Method. The books of account do not reflect any bad debt deduction until a receivable is proven uncollectible.

(2) Advance Provision Method (Allowance for Doubtful Accounts). This method follows the basic accounting concept that expenses should be matched against the related revenue. It is not necessary or desirable to wait for an actual loss before recognizing a bad debt expense on the books. Under this method, an accountant establishes a bad debt expense without knowing which accounts will prove to be worthless. At the time an account is deemed uncollectible, no entry is required to the expense account; instead, a debit is made to the *allowance for doubtful accounts.*

The account allowance for doubtful accounts is called an *offset* or *valuation* account. It appears on the balance sheet immediately after accounts receivable and is deducted from the account. The net result is the estimated realizable value of the accounts receivable.

Methods for Estimating Bad Debts. *Balance Sheet Approach.* 1. *Aging of Accounts Receivable.* 2. *Individual Account Analysis.* The required allowance for doubtful accounts may be determined by analysis of the individual accounts receivable at the end of the accounting period.

(Continued on page 29)

ILLUSTRATIONS AND EXAMPLES

Valuation of Accounts Receivable

1. *Direct Charge-off Method.* The following journal entry is made:

Bad debt expense	100	
Allowance for doubtful accounts		100
To write-off an uncollectible account.		

2. *Advance Provision Method.* The journal entry to record the estimated bad debt expense is:

Bad debt expense	1,200	
Allowance for doubtful accounts		1,200

If a particular account must be written off the following entry is made:

Allowance for doubtful accounts	100	
Accounts receivable–J. Rogers		100

Estimating Bad Debts

Balance Sheet Approach (Aging of Accounts Receivable).

Under this method the trade receivables are classified at the end of the accounting period according to age of the claim. Various percentages are applied to the different age categories (based on prior experience) to determine the estimated uncollectible amount, *i.e.,* the required allowance for doubtful accounts. The percentage uncollectible used for the calculation increases with the length of time the account is past due. It is necessary to take into consideration the existing balance in the allowance account before an adjusting journal entry is made.

Summary of Aged Accounts Receivable

	Amount	Estimated Percentage Uncollectible	Required Allowance for Bad Debts
Not due	$24,000	1	$240
Under 30 days past due	4,600	2	92
Under 60 days past due	2,300	5	115
Under 90 days past due	760	20	152
Over 90 days past due	1,240	75	930
Totals	$32,900		$1,529

If there is a current balance of $457 in the allowance account, the journal entry would be for $1,072 ($1,529 minus $457), Debit: bad debts expense; Credit: allowance for doubtful accounts.

(Continued on page 29)

ANSWERS

11.

June 6	Accounts receivable–P. Jones	3,000	
	Sales		3,000
July 7	Notes receivable–P. Jones	1,880	
	Cash	1,120	
	Accounts receivable–P. Jones		3,000
July 17	Cash	1,882.97	
	Notes receivable		1,880
	Interest income		2.97
	Maturity value (1,880 + 18.80)	*1,898.80*	
	6% for 50 days	*15.83*	
		1,882.97	
Sept. 6	Accounts receivable–P. Jones	1,901.30	
	Cash		1,901.30
	Maturity value	*1,898.80*	
	Protest fees	*2.50*	
		1,901.30	

Answers

F	1
T	2
F	3
F	4
T	5
T	6
T	7
F	8
T	9
F	10

(*Basic Facts continued*)

Income Statement Approach (Percentage of Net Sales). Percentage of net sales may be used as the measure of bad debts expense. In many instances only sales on a credit basis will be taken into consideration for making the computation. This method is not as sophisticated as the balance sheet approach, since external economic factors are given no consideration.

Treatment of Bad Debt Recoveries. After an account has been written off, partial or full collection may occur. At that time the original entry that wrote off the accounts receivable is reversed in the amount recovered.

(Continued on page 30)

(*Illustrations and Examples continued*)

Income Statement Approach (Percentage of Net Sales). One-half of 1% of net sales has been the historical percentage of bad debt losses. If sales totaled $1,000,000, the following entry would be made:

Bad debt expense	5,000	
Allowance for doubtful accounts		5,000

Treatment of Bad Debt Recoveries. Under the direct charge-off method the entry required is: Debit: accounts receivable; Credit bad debt expense. Under the advance provision method the entry is: Debit: account receivable; Credit: allowance for doubtful accounts.

$2,500.00 *New York, N. Y.* *September 4, 19*___

ninety days after date *I* promise to pay

to the order of *Marc Richards*

Twenty-five hundred and 00/100 Dollars

Payable at *Third National Bank and Trust Company*

For value received *with interest at 6%*

J. Rogers

Example of a Notes Receivable

(Continued on page 30)

Notes Receivable. If a customer asks for an extension of time for payment of his open account indebtedness, the creditor may require that a promissory note be issued as evidence of the indebtedness.

Interest Income. The formulas for determination of interest income for a given period can be stated as follows: **principal × interest rate × time = interest.** Rates of interest are usually stated on an annual basis. For ease in computing, a year is presumed to have only 360 days.

Principal × Interest Rate × Time = Interest

interest on $2,000 note at 6% for 2 months

$2,000 × 6% × 60/360 = $20.00

Interest on $5,000 note at 5% for 3 months

$5,000 × 5% × 90/360 = $62.50

End-of-Period Interest Adjustment. At the end of the accounting period, interest must be accrued for all interest-bearing notes still outstanding. The interest on each note must be computed to the balance sheet date.

Discounting the Note—Contingent Liability. Often the payee of a note is unwilling or financially unable to wait until the maturity date to obtain the cash due him. If the note is negotiable, he may *discount* the note at his own bank. This procedure has the effect of liquidating the note receivable. However, the bank will require that the payee make good on the note if the maker defaults. The payee's liability is contingent in nature since he will be called upon to make payment only in the event that the original obligor (maker) does not do so.

Dishonored Notes Held to Maturity by Company. At the time of default an entry is made to transfer the note receivable to an account receivable. If the note is interest-bearing, the interest is treated as being earned and the account receivable includes both the face of the note and the interest.

The Note Discounted Prior to Maturity may be defaulted upon by the maker at maturity.

Notes Receivable

Entries for Recording Notes. When a note is received from a customer with an open account balance, it is necessary to make the following journal entry:

Notes receivable—J. Rogers	2,500	
Accounts receivable—J. Rogers		2,500

To record receipt of 90 day, 6% interest-bearing note in settlement of account receivable.

A company may grant a cash loan to an employee, stockholder, or affiliate and receive a note.

Notes receivable—employees	250	
Cash		250

To record receipt of 30 day non-interest-bearing note from M. Weinstein, salesman.

Collection of Notes. When the note has been presented for collection and payment is made by the maker, the following entry is recorded on the creditor's books:

Cash	2,537.50	
Notes receivable—J. Rogers		2,500.00
Interest income		37.50

To record collection from J. Rogers on December 3, of $2,500 note with interest at 6% for 90 days.

End of Period Interest Adjustment. In the previous illustration, if we closed our books on November 30th, an entry to accrue interest for 87 days would have been made as follows:

Interest receivable	36.25	
Interest income		36.25

If no reversal of the above entry was made, the collection on December 3, would be recorded in the following manner:

Cash	2,537.50	
Notes receivable		2,500.00
Interest receivable		36.25
Interest income		1.25

Discounting the Note—Contingent Liability. The entry to record a discounted note is:

Cash	4,999.23	
Interest expense	.77	
Notes receivable		5,000.00

A $5,000 note, received from John Smith and payable in 90 days from October 1, bearing interest at 5%, is discounted on October 16. Discount rate is 6%.

Face value of note	$5,000.00
Interest on note—90 days @ 5%	62.50
Maturity value	$5,062.50
Discount maturity value—75 days @ 6%	63.27
Proceeds to company	$4,999.23

Discounted Prior to Maturity—If the John Smith note, which was discounted on October 16, is defaulted at maturity, the bank will require payment from the payee. This is recorded as follows:

Accounts receivable—J. Smith	5,062.50	
Cash		5,062.50

8 ACCOUNTING FOR INVENTORY

SELF-TEST

DIRECTIONS: Write your answers (a, b, c, or d) on the numbered lines to the right. To check your answers, turn to page 33.

1. *The method of inventory costing that assumes that the most recent costs are charged against revenue is*
   a first in, first out (fifo)
   b last in, first out (lifo)
   c weighted average method
   d retail method

2. *A method of inventory costing used in the retail trade is*
   a first in, first out (fifo)
   b last in, first out (lifo)
   c weighted average method
   d retail method

3. *In periods of sharply falling prices, the pricing method which yields the lowest inventory valuation is*
   a first in, first out (fifo)
   b last in, first out (lifo)
   c weighted average method
   d retail method

4. *Inventories consist of*
   a merchandise held for sale in the normal course of business
   b supplies consumed in the production of goods and services
   c raw materials, work-in-process, and finished goods
   d all of these

5. *Physical inventories should be taken*
   a in the periodic inventory system *only*
   b in the perpetual inventory system *only*
   c in both the periodic and perpetual inventory systems
   d at year end

QUESTIONS 6, 7, and 8 are based on the following information.
Purchase and sales data related to machine part X-28 for 19___ are as follows:

Purchases		
February 10	20 units @ $ 7.50	$150
April 10	25 units @ 9.00	225
July 1	30 units @ 10.00	300
		$675
Sales		
March 15	15 units @ 12.00	$180
September 5	20 units @ 15.00	300
		$480

6. *The ending inventory consists of*
   a 75 units
   b 60 units
   c 40 units
   d 35 units

7. *The ending inventory computed on the first in, first out (fifo) method is*
   a $330
   b 360
   c 390
   d 675

8. *The weighted average cost per unit is*
   a $7.50
   b 8.00
   c 8.83
   d 9.00

9. *The beginning inventory is $50,000, net purchases for the period total $88,000, and net sales $100,000. Gross profit is estimated at 35%. The merchandise inventory at the end of the period using the gross profit method amounts to*
   a $ 65,000
   b 73,000
   c 100,000
   d 103,000

10. *The lowest inventory valuation in applying the "lower of cost or market rule" is obtained by using*
    a each item
    b each group or category
    c the inventory as a whole
    d none of these

1 ________
2 ________
3 ________
4 ________
5 ________
6 ________
7 ________
8 ________
9 ________
10 ________

BASIC FACTS

Inventories consist of merchandise held for sale in the normal course of business and supplies consumed in producing goods or services. In a manufacturing company, they consist of raw materials, work-in-process, and finished goods.

Periodic and Perpetual Inventory Systems. The quantities of inventories may be determined by one of the two following methods:

(1) The periodic inventory system. At the time of sale, no entries are made charging profit and loss with the cost of merchandise sold. Only the revenue from the sale is recorded. At the end of the accounting period, a physical inventory is taken which enables the determination of the cost of goods sold.

(2) The perpetual inventory system. Inventory increases and decreases are reflected on the books of account and detailed records of quantities are maintained for individual inventory items. Under the perpetual method a physical inventory should be taken at least once a year to confirm the accuracy of the detailed individual records.

Determination of Inventory Quantities. The specific methods involved in taking a physical inventory vary. As a general rule, a physical inventory is taken at least once a year, usually at the end of the accounting period. It is important that all the merchandise in which the business has title is included in the count.

When goods are sold or purchased FOB (free on board) shipping point, title passes at the time delivery is made to a common carrier and goods belong to the purchaser while in transit. If the terms of purchase or sale are FOB destination, then title does not pass until the goods reach their destination. It is necessary to examine both sales and purchase invoices for a few days surrounding the last day of the accounting period to reveal if there are purchases or sales in transit, which must be added or deleted from the inventory.

Determination of Cost. The American Institute of Certified Public Accountants defines inventory costs as "the sum of the applicable expenditures and charges directly or indirectly incurred in bringing an article to its existing condition and location." Cost, therefore, will include not only the invoice price of an article but such related items as transportation, insurance, customs duties, and purchasing costs. The preferred treatment of purchase discounts is as a reduction of inventory cost.

Cost Methods. A practical problem of inventory costing is that identical items may have been purchased at varying prices. At the end of the accounting period, a cost must be assigned to the quantities remaining in the inventory. If it is not possible to identify the specific item with its actual cost (this method is called specific identification), then a method of determining the *flow of costs* must be adopted. Several assumptions as to the flow of costs meet generally accepted accounting principles. An enterprise should adopt the method that will most clearly reflect periodic income.

First In, First Out (fifo). Costs are charged against revenue in the order in which they were incurred. This method reflects the ending inventory at the current value, as indicated by the most recent purchases.

(*Continued on page 34*)

ILLUSTRATIONS AND EXAMPLES

Determination of Costs

The use of a perpetual inventory is assumed in the solution.

Purchases		
March 1	25 units @ $10	$250
June 10	20 units @ 7	140
September 15	30 units @ 12	360
		$750
Sales		
April 10	15 units @ $15	$225
December 12	20 units @ 20	400
		$625

There are 40 units on hand at December 31.

First In, First Out. Under this method the 40 units in the ending inventory are assumed to consist of the following:

June 10	10 units @ $ 7	$ 70
September 15	30 units @ 12	360
Ending inventory, fifo		$430

Revenues are charged with $320 of cost ($750–$430); gross profit on sales is $305 ($625–$320).

(*Continued on page 34*)

EXPLANATIONS

1. *The method of inventory costing that assumes that the most recent costs are charged against revenue is* last in, first out (lifo). The lifo method assumes that the most recently acquired goods are sold first. This assumption is not related to the physical flow of goods, but to the flow of costs entering into the revenue cycle.

2. *A method of inventory costing used in the retail trade* is the retail method, used with a periodic inventory system by many retail businesses. Inventory is counted and priced at retail. The reduction to cost is made by applying to the retail value a percentage arrived at by computing the cost of purchases to their retail prices.

3. *In periods of sharply falling prices, the pricing method which yields the lowest inventory valuation* is first in, first out (fifo). Under the fifo method, the oldest costs are charged to cost of goods sold first, leaving the most recent costs in inventory.

4. *Inventories consist of* raw materials, work-in-process, and finished goods in manufacturing businesses. The AICPA definition of inventory also includes items of tangible personal property which are to be currently consumed in the production of goods or services to be available for sale.

5. *Physical inventories should be taken* in both the periodic and perpetual inventory systems. In the periodic system, inventory must be taken at the year end to determine the quantity of goods on hand. Under the perpetual inventory system, a physical count should be taken sometime during the year to determine the accuracy and reliability of the perpetual records.

6. *The ending inventory consists of* 40 units. Total purchases, in units, amounted to 75. Sales totaled 35 units leaving a balance of 40.

7. *The ending inventory computed on the first in, first out (fifo) method is* $390. Fifo assumes that the first costs incurred are the first to enter the revenue cycle. This means that the ending inventory would be comprised of the last costs incurred.

30 units purchased on July 1	@ $10	$300
10 units purchased on April 10	@ 9	90
40		$390

8. *The weighted average cost per unit is* $9.00. Weighted average method assumes that costs enter the revenue cycle on an average basis. The total cost of the units acquired is divided by the number of units purchased. The 75 units had a total cost of $675, for an average cost of $9.00.

9. *The beginning inventory is $50,000, net purchases for the period total $88,000 and net sales $100,000. Gross profit is estimated at 35%. The merchandise inventory at the end of the period using the gross profit method amounts to $73,000.*

Merchandise inventory, beginning of period		$ 50,000
Purchase (net)		88,000
Merchandise available for sale		$138,000
Sales for the period	$100,000	
Less: estimated gross profit (35% of $100,000)	35,000	
Estimated cost of goods sold		65,000
Estimated inventory, end of period		$73,000

10. *The lowest inventory valuation in applying the "lower of cost or market rule"* is obtained by using each item. The inventory valuation obtained by applying the lower of cost or market rule to each item will never exceed the total obtained by the other two methods: the group method or the inventory as a whole.

Answers

b	1
d	2
a	3
d	4
c	5
c	6
c	7
d	8
b	9
a	10

Last In, First Out (lifo). The most recent costs are charged against revenue. The year end inventory consists of items valued at their earliest costs which, in periods of sharply rising prices, will result in a low valuation on the balance sheet. Current costs are matched against current sales prices.

Weighted Average Method (Average Cost). Costs are charged against revenues on the basis of a computed average. Weighted averages are determined by dividing the total costs incurred in acquiring the units available for sale by the total number of units.

Lower of Cost or Market Rule. Cost is the basic method of valuing inventory. However, it is also necessary to determine "market," since there may exist a decline in value of inventory items. Market generally connotes replacement cost of the merchandise on the inventory date. A decline in cost price should be recognized in the period when incurred. Market is further restricted in that it should not exceed the estimated selling price less cost of disposal and not be less than the estimated selling price less cost of disposal and an allowance for a normal profit margin.

Retail Method of Valuing Inventory. In the retail trade it is often difficult to determine the cost of the merchandise under the conventional cost methods. Instead, the inventory is taken at the retail prices and converted to cost by applying the ratio prevailing between cost and retail during the period. Advantages of this method are: (1) it does not require a physical inventory for the preparation of interim financial statements; and (2) individual cost of items need not be determined, thus much record-keeping is eliminated.

Gross Profit Method of Estimating Inventories. Since taking a physical inventory is costly and time-consuming, it is usually done only once a year. Management, on the other hand, may require a monthly financial statement. Inventory for interim statements is usually estimated by the gross profit method. This method is also used to establish the dollar amount of merchandise destroyed by fire. The method uses an estimate of the gross profit realized on sales for the period determined historically or empirically.

Last In, First Out. The April 10th sale of 15 units came from the March 1st purchase. As of December 12th, the inventory consisted of the following:

March 1	10 units @ $10	$100
June 10	20 units @ 7	140
September 15	30 units @ 12	360
		$600

The December 12th sale of 20 units would be from the September 15th layer and the ending inventory consists of 40 units costed below:

March 1	10 units @ $10	$100
June 10	20 units @ 7	140
September 15	10 units @ 12	120
Ending inventory, lifo		$360

Revenues are charged with $390 of cost ($750–$360); gross profit on sales is $235 ($625–$390).

Weighted Average Method (Average Cost). A weighted average cost is determined for the purchases for the year.

March 1	25 units @ $10	$250
June 10	20 units @ 7	140
September 15	30 units @ 12	360
	75 units	$750
	Weighted Average Unit Cost	$ 10

The ending inventory is valued at $400. Revenues are charged with $350 ($750–$400); gross profit on sales is $275 ($625–$350).

Retail Method of Valuing Inventory.

	Cost	Retail
Merchandise inventory, beginning of period . .	$ 20,000	$ 32,000
Purchases (net).	85,000	125,500
Merchandise available for sale	$105,000	$157,500
Less: sales for period		117,500
Merchandise inventory, end of period at retail price.		$ 40,000

Ratio between cost and retail of merchandise available for sale ($105,000 ÷ $157,500) 66 2/3%

Merchandise inventory, end of period at cost (66 2/3% × $40,000) $26,667.

Gross Profit Method. The beginning inventory amounts to $25,000, net purchases for the period $20,000 and net sales $30,000. The gross profit is estimated at 40%.

Merchandise inventory, beginning of period		$25,000
Purchases (net).		20,000
Merchandise available for sale		45,000
Sales for period	$30,000	
Less: estimated gross profit ($30,000 × 40%)	12,000	
Estimated cost of goods sold		18,000
Estimated merchandise inventory, end of period.		$27,000

9 FIXED ASSETS I

SELF-TEST

1. On January 1, 19___ a new machine having a five-year life is purchased at a cost of $50,000. Compute the annual depreciation expense and the balance in the accumulated depreciation account for the five-year period using the following methods (assume no salvage value):
   Straight Line
   Sum of Years Digits
   Double Declining Balance

2. A truck is purchased for cash in the amount of $7,327. The itemized invoice shows:

Truck	$6,400
Sales tax (3%)	192
Insurance for one year	500
License fees for one year	85
Spare tires	150
	$7,327

Record the journal entry for the acquisition of the truck. TO CHECK your answers, turn to page 37.

BASIC FACTS

Definition and Classifications. Tangible fixed assets are long-lived assets used in the operations of a business. They are not intended for sale in the normal course of business. Therefore, such items as land held for sale or idle buildings and equipment are not fixed assets. Tangible fixed assets can be grouped as follows:

a. Subject to depreciation (buildings, machinery, equipment, furniture and automobiles).
b. Subject to depletion (mines, oil wells, timber).
c. Not subject to depreciation or depletion (land).

Recording the Cost of Fixed Assets. Fixed assets are recorded at their *original cost*. Cost includes all expenditures related to acquisition, and charges for placing the asset in its proper location and making it operative. Items which require capitalization (inclusion in cost) are: invoice cost less cash and trade discounts; transportation costs; insurance while in transit; sales and excise taxes and duties; and initial installation costs. There is an overriding condition that the cost must be *reasonable* and *necessary*.

In the case of land, certain additional costs are capitalized, such as real estate commissions, escrow and title fees, professional fees, and assessments. If land is acquired with an unwanted building, the cost of demolition is also included in land cost.

Where an asset is constructed for use in the business, a portion of the overhead expenses should be capitalized along with the material and labor costs. Certain expenditures during construction, if material, should be considered for capitalization (e.g., insurance expense, interest charges, and architectural fees). It should be remembered that where cost of construction is less than the cost of acquisition from outsiders the asset should be carried at the lesser cost of construction. A serious accounting problem exists where the cost to purchase is less than the cost of construction. It is probable that the lower figure would be used, under the theory that the higher figure incorporated various operating inefficiencies.

Depreciation Accounting. The purpose of depreciation is to allocate the cost of a fixed asset over the years of productive use. A depreciation policy is a systematic and logical method of allocating fixed asset costs to the

(*Continued on page 38*)

ILLUSTRATIONS AND EXAMPLES

Depreciation Methods.

Machine cost	$ 16,000
Estimated scrap value	$ 1,000
Estimated useful life	5 years
Estimated number of units produced	300,000

Year 1	75,000 units
Year 2	70,000 units
Year 3	50,000 units
Year 4	55,000 units
Year 5	50,000 units
	300,000 units

The Straight Line Method is computed by the following formula:

$$\frac{\text{Cost less Estimated Scrap Value}}{\text{Estimated Useful Life}} = \text{Depreciation}$$

$$\frac{\$16{,}000 - \$1{,}000}{5 \text{ years}} = \$3{,}000$$

The annual depreciation charge for the 5-year period would be $3,000.00 per year.

Sum of Years Digits Method provides for a progressively declining depreciation charge and is calculated in the following manner:

1. A fraction is computed for a given year.
2. The numerator is the number of years of remaining asset life at the beginning of the accounting period.
3. The denominator is the sum total of years for all accounting periods.

Year	Amount Depreciated (Cost Less Scrap Value)	Depreciation Rate	Depreciation
1	$15,000	5/15	$5,000
2	15,000	4/15	4,000
3	15,000	3/15	3,000
4	15,000	2/15	2,000
5	15,000	1/15	1,000

Declining Balance Method, similar to the sum of years digits method, provides for increased depreciation charges in the earlier years of the asset's life. Both methods have met with considerable favor for several reasons. There is widespread business opinion that assets lose more economic value in the earlier years and that the depreciation method adopted should reflect this factor. In our highly developed society, technological changes are so rapid that there is a tendency to overstate the asset's life. Therefore, the use of a declining depreciation method is justified. It may also be pointed out that there is a considerable tax advantage to the utilization of declining amount methods.

(*Continued on page 38*)

ANSWERS

1.

Straight Line Computation:

$$\frac{\text{Cost}}{\text{Estimated Useful Life}} = \frac{\$50{,}000}{5} = \$10{,}000 \text{ annual depreciation}$$

Year	Depreciation Expense	Accumulated Depreciation
1	$10,000	$10,000
2	10,000	20,000
3	10,000	30,000
4	10,000	40,000
5	10,000	50,000

Sum of Years Digits Computation:

Year	Depreciation Rate	Depreciation Expense	Accumulated Depreciation
1	5/15	$16,667	$16,667
2	4/15	13,333	30,000
3	3/15	10,000	40,000
4	2/15	6,667	46,667
5	1/15	3,333	50,000

Double Declining Balance Computation:

Year	Cost	Accumulated Depreciation at Beginning of Year	Amount to be Depreciated	Rate	Depreciation Expense	Accumulated Depreciation
1	$50,000	—	$50,000	40%	$20,000	$20,000
2	50,000	20,000	30,000	40%	12,000	32,000
3	50,000	32,000	18,000	40%	7,200	39,200
4	50,000	39,200	10,800	40%	4,320	43,520
5	50,000	43,520	6,480	40%	2,592	46,112

2.

	Debit	Credit
Truck	6,742	
Prepaid insurance	500	
Prepaid taxes	85	
Cash		7,327

To record acquisition of truck. Sales tax and spare tires should be included as part of the original cost of the truck. The insurance and license fees items may be charged to an expense account rather than a prepaid asset.

accounting periods benefited. Therefore the cost of fixed assets is matched against revenue. It is a misconception to consider depreciation as a valuation method. Since fixed assets are reflected at cost, the net book value represents merely the unallocated cost which will be charged to future accounting periods. The market value, at any given date, would not necessarily bear any relation to the undepreciated cost.

The major reasons for tangible fixed assets having limited life are physical deterioration and obsolescence. In the determination of the estimated useful life of an asset, the primary reason for depreciation is the governing factor. Depreciation does not represent a cash expenditure and the accumulated depreciation does not provide funds for replacement of the asset.

Depreciation Methods. Several factors must be considered in the determination of the depreciation expense for a given accounting period. These include cost, estimated salvage value, and estimated life (measured by time periods, units of production, or machine hours). The latter factors, since they are estimates, must be based on engineering studies, management evaluation, and Internal Revenue Service guidelines. The depreciation methods most commonly used are *straight line, sum of years digits, declining balance,* and *units of production.*

Recording Depreciation. The methods of computing depreciation may result in very diverse charges being made to the income account for the accounting period. The journal entry to record depreciation, however, is not affected by the choice of depreciation method. Depreciation expense is debited and accumulated depreciation is credited for the amount of the depreciation expense for the period. The accumulated depreciation account is known as a *contra asset* account; it appears on the balance sheet as a deduction from the related asset account.

The double declining balance method (200% of straight-line) is illustrated as follows:

Year	Cost	Accumulated Depreciation at Beginning of Year	Amount to be Depre-cited	Rate	Depreciation for Year
1	$16,000	—	$16,000.00	40%	$6,400.00
2	16,000	$ 6,400.00	9,600.00	40%	3,840.00
3	16,000	10,240.00	5,760.00	40%	2,304.00
4	16,000	12,544.00	3,456.00	40%	1,382.40
5	16,000	13,926.40	2,073.60	40%	829.44

From the above tabulation, certain differences between the declining balance method and the straight line and sum of years digits methods become apparent. Salvage value is not considered in the depreciable base because the method provides for a built-in residual value. The depreciable amount does not remain constant as it does in the methods previously illustrated. Under the double declining method the amount to be depreciated is always reduced by the accumulated depreciation taken in previous years.

Units of Production Method attempts to relate the expired cost to production units rather than time periods. The formula for the yearly depreciation charge is as follows:

$$\frac{\text{Cost less Salvage Value}}{\text{Estimated Units of Production}} \times \text{Annual Units of Production}$$

The unit depreciation is calculated as follows:

$$\frac{\$16{,}000 - \$1{,}000}{300{,}000} = \$.05 \text{ per unit}$$

Year	Number of Units Produced	Depreciation
1	75,000	$3,750
2	70,000	3,500
3	50,000	2,500
4	55,000	2,750
5	50,000	2,500

This method has found limited favor in actual practice.

10 FIXED ASSETS II

SELF-TEST

DIRECTIONS: For questions 1–6, write your answers (a, b, c, or d) on the numbered lines to the right. To check your answers, turn to page **41**.

1. *Goodwill is an asset representing*
   a the unrecorded value of a trade name
   b the present value of future earnings in excess of normal earnings prevalent in a particular industry
   c the unrecorded appreciation in the value of fixed assets above their cost
   d the favorable reputation of a company

2. *An entry appears on the books of the Paird and William Company debiting accumulated depreciation–automobiles $3,200, and crediting automobiles for $3,200. The reason for this entry is*
   a the abandonment of a fully depreciated automobile
   b the sale of an automobile for cash
   c to record the annual depreciation expense
   d to record an extraordinary repair to the automobile

3. *According to the Internal Revenue Code, gains and losses arising from the exchange of similar property*
   a should be recognized
   b should not be recognized, but an adjustment should be made to the basis of the acquired property
   c should not be recognized, but an adjustment should be made to depreciation expense
   d should not be recognized, but an adjustment should be made to accumulated depreciation

4. *Costs charged to an asset account or to accumulated depreciation are considered to be*
   a expensed
   b capitalized
   c revenue expenditure
   d extraordinary charge

5. *The cost of intangibles such as copyrights, patents, and leaseholds*
   a should be written off to expense at time of acquisition
   b should be carried on the books for the entire existence of the business entity
   c should be written down to a nominal value such as $1.
   d should be amortized over the useful life of the asset by periodic charges against revenue

6. *A printing press with a cost of $15,000 and accumulated depreciation of $12,000 is sold for $5,000. The correct journal entry to record the transaction is*

a	Accumulated depreciation	12,000	
	Cash	5,000	
	Machinery		15,000
	Gain on sale of machinery		2,000
b	Cash	5,000	
	Machinery		5,000
c	Cash	5,000	
	Accumulated depreciation	12,000	
	Machinery		17,000
d	None of the above		

In the left-hand column are listed eight examples of business assets. In the right-hand column are five classes of fixed assets and a sixth choice "not a fixed asset." Determine the category into which each asset falls, and indicate by writing a–f on the numbered lines to the right.

7. *Land in use as a building site*
8. *Patent*
9. *Growing timber*
10. *Bowling equipment in hands of manufacturer*
11. *Idle building, held for sale*
12. *Perpetual franchise*
13. *Furniture and fixtures*
14. *Plots of land held for speculation*

a Tangible fixed asset subject to depreciation
b Tangible fixed asset not subject to depreciation
c Natural resources
d Intangible fixed asset having limited existence
e Intangible fixed asset having indefinite life
f Not a fixed asset

1 ______
2 ______
3 ______
4 ______
5 ______
6 ______
7 ______
8 ______
9 ______
10 ______
11 ______
12 ______
13 ______
14 ______

BASIC FACTS

Capitalized *Vs.* Revenue Expenditures. In accounting for fixed assets those expenditures which are properly charged to an asset account must be distinguished from those which should be charged against revenues as an expense. Capitalized to an asset account are:

1. Those expenditures that represent the acquisition cost of a new asset, including the invoice cost of the asset, transportation, and installation charges.
2. Those expenditures that add additional efficiency, life, or capacity to an asset. These items include the cost of new construction to an existing building and the cost of rewiring a building to increase its electrical capacity.

Ordinary repairs are properly chargeable to expense. In many instances, companies will establish minimum dollar amounts for the capitalization of expenditures to an asset account. Repairs of an extraordinary nature, which increase the estimated useful life of an asset, are properly treated as capital expenditures. The general treatment is to debit the appropriate accumulated depreciation account rather than the asset account. The effect in either case is the same—an increase in the net book value of the asset.

Asset Disposal. At some time, every fixed asset will wear out or become obsolete and the company will dispose of it by one of three general ways: *abandonment, sale, trade-in.*

Abandonment. It is merely necessary to remove the cost and the related accumulated depreciation from the books of account. Any undepreciated cost is treated as a loss on abandonment.

Sale. It is unusual for the sales price to agree with the book value of the asset at the date of sale. This means that a gain or loss on the sale will have to be recognized on the books of account. The computation of the gain or loss is done by subtracting the net book value of the asset from the sales price. A positive result indicates a gain; a negative result means that a loss was sustained.

Trade-in. Where an asset is traded-in, it is customary for the seller to grant an allowance to the buyer. This trade-in allowance has the effect of reducing the cash required to purchase the new asset and will usually bear no relationship to the value of the asset as it is carried on the books. The trade-in allowance may be established at a higher amount than the actual fair market value of the asset to be exchanged. The seller has, in effect, granted the buyer a discount from the list price of the new asset. The Internal Revenue Code states that for tax purposes no gain or loss is recognized on the exchange of similar

(Continued on page 41)

ILLUSTRATIONS AND EXAMPLES

Asset Disposal

Abandonment. If a machine which cost $1,000 and which was fully depreciated is abandoned, the following entry is made:

Accumulated depreciation—plant equipment	1,000	
Plant equipment		1,000

Sale. A machine with a cost of $25,000 and which was depreciated to the extent of $12,000 was sold for $15,000. The book value on the date of sale is $13,000 ($25,000–$12,000) and the gain on the sale is $2,000. The entry to record the sale is:

Cash	15,000	
Accumulated depreciation—plant equipment	12,000	
Plant equipment		25,000
Gain on sale of fixed assets		2,000

Trade-in. Assume that an automobile with an original cost of $4,800 and on which depreciation of $4,200 has been taken has been traded in for a new model. The invoice price of the new automobile is $5,000 and the dealer grants the purchaser a trade-in allowance of $1,000 on the old automobile. The new automobile will be carried on the books at $4,600, computed in the following manner:

Cost of old automobile	4,800
Depreciation taken to date of trade-in	4,200
Book value of old automobile	600
Cash required to purchase new automobile ($5,000 - $1,000)	4,000
Basis of new automobile	4,600

The bookkeeping entry to record the transaction is:

Automobile (new)	4,600	
Accumulated depreciation—automobile	4,200	
Automobile (old)		4,800
Cash		4,000

The alternative method, assuming the trade-in allowance of $1,000 to be the fair market value of the old automobile, is to recognize the gain of $400 on the trade-in and record the new automobile at $5,000.

EXPLANATIONS

1. *Goodwill is an asset representing* the present value of future earnings in excess of normal earnings prevalent in a particular industry. There is more than one method of computing goodwill, each requiring the use of subjective valuations.

2. *An entry appears on the books of the Paird and William Company debiting accumulated depreciation–automobiles $3,200, and crediting automobiles for $3,200. The reason for this entry is* the abandonment of a fully depreciated automobile. A debt to the accumulated depreciation account with an offsetting credit to the asset account is made when a fully depreciated asset is abandoned. A fully depreciated asset will not be written off as long as it is used in the operation of the business.

3. *According to the Internal Revenue Code, gains and losses arising from the exchange of similar property* should not be recognized, but an adjustment should be made to the basis of the acquired property.

4. *Costs charged to an asset account or to accumulated depreciation are considered to be* capitalized. They differ from revenue expenditures, which benefit only the current accounting period, in that they are intended to benefit future periods. Additions to fixed assets are debited to the asset account, expenditures that increase the useful life of an existing asset are debited to the accumulated depreciation account.

5. *The cost of intangibles such as copyrights, patents, and leaseholds* should be amortized over the useful life of the asset by periodic charges against revenue. This is accomplished by means of amortization.

6. *A printing press with a cost of $15,000 and accumulated depreciation of $12,000 is sold for $5,000. The correct journal entry to record the transaction is:*

Accumulation depreciation	12,000	
Cash	5,000	
Machinery		15,000
Gain on sale of machinery		2,000

When an asset is sold, gain or loss is recognized. The asset account and the accumulated depreciation account are both closed out. The gain or loss is determined by subtracting the net book value from the cash received.

Answers

b	1
a	2
b	3
b	4
d	5
a	6
b	7
d	8
c	9
f	10
f	11
e	12
a	13
f	14

(Basic Facts Continued)

property. The often arbitrary nature of the trade-in allowance has prompted many companies to adopt the tax treatment for accounting purposes. This treatment results in carrying the value of the new asset at a price different from the list or invoice price.

Subsidiary Ledgers–Fixed Assets. Where the number of fixed asset items is significant, or where depreciation is computed on a unit by unit basis, good accounting control requires the establishment of a plant ledger. This is a subsidiary record which will provide the details of the fixed asset account in the general ledger.

The plant ledger provides the information necessary to determine the depreciation expense for an accounting period, provides a basis for the support of an insurance claim, and acts as a control over physical existence of the assets.

Intangible Assets. The designation *intangible assets* is given to those business assets which have no physical characteristics, but which give to the business entity certain legal rights or competitive advantages. Examples are: copyrights, patents, franchises,

(Continued on page 42)

trademarks, leaseholds, and goodwill. In addition to being non-physical in nature, these assets cannot be of the type classified as a current asset. This eliminates such items as accounts receivable and prepaid expenses from inclusion in the intangible category.

Intangibles should be valued at their cost to the business enterprise. If the intangible asset did not arise from a cost of acquisition or of development, its existence is not recognized on the books of account.

The accounting treatment of intangible assets is different for each of the two general groups of intangible assets.

Type A are intangibles having a limited useful life such as copyrights, patents, and leaseholds. The cost of the assets is amortized over the useful life of the asset by periodic charges against revenue. The legal or contractual life should be used for the amortization period unless it can be established that the use of a shorter life is more realistic.

Type B are intangibles having unlimited useful life such as goodwill, organization costs, and perpetual franchises. The cost of these assets should be carried on the books for the entire existence of the business entity or until there is evidence of limited useful life.

Goodwill. Goodwill is an intangible asset, representing the cost of a purchased business in excess of the net fair market value of its assets. The goodwill represents the present value of future earnings in excess of normal earnings prevalent in the particular industry. The excess earnings may be due to management skills, location, reputation, etc. Several methods mav be employed in the determination of such goodwill, including:

1. An arbitrary amount agreed to by both buyer and seller.
2. A multiple of the average profits for past years.
3. A multiple of the amount of annual earnings above the normal earnings.
4. The capitalized value of the excess earnings, using the normal capitalization rate for the industry.

Depletion—Natural Resources. Natural resources are assets which are depleted and therefore their cost is allocated by *periodic* charges to income. Depletion expense for a given accounting period is determined by the following formula:

$$\frac{\text{Cost of the natural resource less salvage value}}{\text{Estimated total deposit (units, tons, barrel, etc.)}} \times \text{Amount of deposit removed during accounting period} = \text{Depletion Expense}$$

The entry for depletion is similar to that for depreciation and the balance sheet presentation parallels that of plant assets.

11

PARTNERSHIPS I

SELF-TEST

On January 1, Greenberg and Pepper formed a partnership in which Greenberg invested $60,000 and Pepper $40,000. The capital accounts for the year are as follows:

W. Greenberg	
	1/1 60,000
	7/1 20,000

J. Pepper	
	1/1 40,000
	9/1 27,000
	12/1 12,000

Partnership income for the year amounted to $30,000. How would the net income be distributed to the partners under each of the following conditions? (To check your answers, turn to page **45**.)

1. *The partnership agreement said nothing about the distribution of net income.*

2. *The partnership agreement provided that Greenberg and Pepper share net income in a 70–30 ratio respectively.*

3. *The partnership agreement provided that the partners share net income in accordance with the ratio of their beginning capital.*

4. *The partnership agreement provided that the partners share net income in accordance with their average capital ratio.*

5. *The partnership agreement provided that Greenberg would be allowed a salary of $5,000 and Pepper a salary of $3,000, the balance of net income would be distributed equally.*

6. *The partnership agreement provided that Greenberg would be allowed a salary of $4,000 and Pepper $3,500; that interest at 6% would be allowed on beginning capital; and that the balance would be distributed equally.*

BASIC FACTS

A Partnership is "an association of two or more persons to carry on, as co-owners, a business for profit" (The Uniform Partnership Act). Some of the attributes of a partnership are:

Unlimited liability. Each general partner is individually liable for all of the obligations of the partnership.

Limited life. The life of a partnership may be terminated by the voluntary act of a partner or by such involuntary acts as bankruptcy, death, or incapacity of a partner.

Entity. A partnership is not a separate entity from its individual members.

Co-ownership of profits and property. Property invested in a partnership becomes jointly owned by all of the partners. An individual partner has an equity in the total assets of the partnership but no individual right to any specific asset. Partnership profits are divided among the partners in an agreed-upon ratio. Each partner has a right of ownership in the profits.

Partner's Investment. A general journal entry is made to record each partner's contribution to the partnership. If a partner contributes assets other than cash as part or all of his investment, the value of these non-cash items must be determined. Sound accounting treatment requires that the *fair market value* of each asset be established and used on the books of account of the partnership. Each asset is debited in an appropriate ledger account; any liabilities assumed by the partnership would be set up in a credit account; and the net value of the assets contributed would be credited to the individual partner's *capital account*. This procedure is also followed for any additional investments made by the partners.

Partner's Drawing. During the year each partner will be withdrawing partnership assets for his personal use. Some common transactions of this type include the partner's cash drawings, direct payment by the partnership of personal liabilities, and the appropriation of partnership inventory for personal use. These transactions could all be charged to the partner by debiting the individual capital account.

(*Continued on page 46*)

ILLUSTRATIONS AND EXAMPLES

Partner's Investment

Cash	5,000	
Building	60,000	
Furniture	8,000	
Mortgage payable		13,000
Richard Adams, capital		60,000

To record investment made by Richard Adams in Adams and Roberts, a partnership.

Sharing the Income or Loss

The illustrations will assume the capital accounts in the following amounts:

Richard Adams, Capital		Louis Roberts, Capital	
	1/1 27,000		1/1 9,000
	7/1 4,000		3/1 7,200
	9/1 3,000		

Partnership income for the year was $16,000.

Fixed Ratio of Income. If Adams and Roberts share profits in a ratio of 6 to 4, it means that Adams receives 60% of the partnership net income; Roberts is credited with 40%. The applicable percentages are applied to the net income and Adams would be credited with $9,600 ($16,000 x 60%) and Roberts $6,400.

Capital Ratio

Based on Beginning Capital

	Amount	% of total
Adams' beginning capital is	$27,000	75%
Roberts' beginning capital is	9,000	25%
Total beginning capital	$36,000	100%

Adams would, therefore, be credited with $12,000 ($16,000 x 75%); Roberts with $4,000.

Based on Average Capital

Adams' Average Capital

January 1 to June 30	27,000 X 6 months =	$162,000
July 1 to August 31	31,000 X 2 months =	62,000
September 1 to December 31	34,000 X 4 months =	136,000
Total		$360,000
Average capital (360,000 ÷ 12)		= $ 30,000

Roberts' Average Capital

January 1 to February 28	9,000 X 2 months =	$ 18,000
March 1 to December 31	16,200 X 10 months =	162,000
Total		= $180,000
Average capital (180,000 ÷ 12)		$ 15,000
Combined total		$ 45,000

Under this method Adams would be credited with 66-2/3% of the profit $\left(\frac{30,000}{45,000} \times 16,000\right)$ or $10,667; Roberts' share is 33-1/3% or $5,333.

(*Continued on page 46*)

ANSWERS

1.

Greenberg's share	$15,000
Pepper's share	15,000
Total	$30,000

If nothing is said in the agreement the partners share equally.

2.

Greenberg's share (70% × $30,000)	$21,000
Pepper's share (30% × $30,000)	9,000
Total	$30,000

3.

Greenberg's share (60% × $30,000)	$18,000
Pepper's share (40% × $30,000)	12,000
Total	$30,000

Capital account-January 1, 19__

Greenberg	$ 60,000	60%
Pepper	40,000	40%
	$100,000	100%

4. Greenberg's Average Capital

January 1, 19__-June 30, 19__	$60,000 x 6 months =	$360,000
July 1, 19__-December 31, 19__	80,000 x 6 months =	480,000
		$840,000
Average Capital ($840,000 ÷ 12)		$ 70,000

Pepper's Average Capital

January 1, 19__-August 31, 19__	$40,000 x 8 months =	$320,000
September 1, 19__-Nov. 30, 19__	67,000 x 3 months =	201,000
December 1, 19__-December 31, 19__	79,000 x 1 month =	79,000
		$600,000

Average capital ($600,000 ÷ 12)	$ 50,000	
Total average capital ($70,000 + 50,000)	$120,000	
Greenberg's share (70/120 x $30,000)		$ 17,500
Pepper's share (50/120 x $30,000)		12,500
		$ 30,000

5.

Net income to be divided		$30,000
Partners' salary allocations		
to Greenberg	$5,000	
to Pepper	3,000	8,000
Balance to be divided equally		$22,000

	Salary	Remainder	Total
Greenberg	$5,000	$11,000	$16,000
Pepper	3,000	11,000	14,000
Totals	$8,000	$22,000	$30,000

6.

Net income to be divided			$30,000
Partners' salary allocations			
to Greenberg	$4,000		
to Pepper	3,500	$7,500	
Interest on invested capital (beginning)			
Greenberg (6% x $60,000)	$3,600		
Pepper (6% x $40,000)	2,400	6,000	13,500
Remaining balance to be divided equally			$16,500

	Total	Salary	Interest	Remainder
Greenberg	$15,850	$4,000	$3,600	$ 8,250
Pepper	14,150	3,500	2,400	8,250
Totals	$30,000	$7,500	$6,000	$16,500

However, it is customary to reflect the permanent capital and the current drawings in separate accounts.

Sharing the Income or Loss. Individual partners are not employees of their partnership. Their remuneration is determined by allocating to each a share of the net income or loss of the partnership. This net income consists of three elements: (1) a return to the partnership for the personal services of the partners; (2) a return to the partnership for the use of the capital invested; and (3) the residual profit generated by the business. It would be logical to allocate the net income equally among the partners only when each partner has made equal contributions. In many cases the partners are not equal as to the amount of time they devote to the partnership activities or in the amount of their invested capital. Since these items affect the first two elements of partnership income, it is reasonable that certain adjustments be made to the partner's allocable shares to compensate for these disparities. Following are some of the methods used to adjust partner inequalities:

Fixed Ratio of Income. Each partner receives a fixed percentage of the net income of the partnership, as set forth in the partnership agreement. If no agreement as to division of profits exists, profits are shared equally.

Capital Ratio. Where a large amount of capital is necessary for partnership earnings and where the personal services of the partners is not the dominant income-producing factor, then a ratio based on partners' capital investment is often used. Since capital investment is sometimes increased or decreased during the year, there must be agreement between the partners as to how capital should be defined for purposes of the calculation.

The use of the *beginning capital account* is the simplest method to apply. This method has the disadvantage of giving no weight to contributions made by partners after the beginning of the year. This can be overcome by using an *average capital ratio*.

Recognizing Salaries and Interest Factors. A more complex division can be utilized where services and capital investment both are disproportionate. Profits can be charged with an agreed amount for partners' salaries and for interest on capital investment. These charges *are not expenses* of the partnership and therefore do not affect the partnership profits; they are merely devices or methods used to apportion profits. After the salaries and interest are charged against the profits, the balance is divided in a fixed ratio.

Recognizing Salaries and Interest Factors. Assume that Adams is entitled to a salary of $5,000 and Roberts to a salary of $8,000 and that interest is to be allowed on the January 1 capital balance at the rate of 5% per annum. The net income would be distributed as follows:

Net income to be divided			16,000
Partners' salary allocations			
to Adams	5,000		
to Roberts	8,000	13,000	
Interest on beginning invested capital			
Adams–(27,000 × .05)	$1,350		
Roberts–(9,000 × .05)	450	1,800	14,800
Remaining balance to be divided equally			$1,200
Adams	$ 600		
Roberts	600		$1,200

The amount distributed to each partner can be summarized:

	Total	Salary	Interest	Remainder
Richard Adams	$ 6,950	$ 5,000	$1,350	$ 600
Louis Roberts	9,050	8,000	450	600
Totals	$16,000	$13,000	$1,800	$1,200

12 PARTNERSHIPS II

SELF-TEST

DIRECTIONS: For questions 1–6, write your answers (a, b, c, or d) on the numbered lines to the right. To check your answers, turn to page 49.

1. *X, Y, and Z are partners sharing profits in a ratio of 40%, 40% and 20% respectively. The partnership has been liquidated and after payment to all creditors $40,000 of cash remains available for distribution among the partners. Partner X has a capital account balance of $30,000, Partner Y has a capital account balance of $20,000, Partner Z, who is personally bankrupt, has a debit capital balance of $10,000. How much cash will Partner X receive?*
   a $40,000
   b 30,000
   c 25,000
   d 16,000

2. *A new partner may be admitted to a partnership*
   a with the consent of any one partner
   b with the consent of all the old partners
   c with the consent of two-thirds of the old partners
   d by making an investment

3. *Marc has purchased Richard's interest in the partnership of Adam and Richard for $25,000. Richard's capital account shows a balance of $20,000 at the time of acquisition. The following should be recorded on the partnership's books*
   a goodwill should be recorded for $5,000
   b Adam's capital account should be increased by $5,000
   c Richard's capital balance of $20,000 should be transferred to Marc
   d assets should be reduced by $5,000

4. *In the liquidation of a partnership, gains or losses resulting from the sale of operating assets should be divided among the partners*
   a in the partnership capital ratio
   b in the same ratio as operating income or losses
   c in the ratio of the partners' original capital contribution
   d equally

5. *On the partnership books, if a bonus is given to a new partner to acknowledge the existence of certain special personal attributes*
   a goodwill is recognized
   b assets existing on the partnership books should be revalued
   c the old partners are charged for the bonus
   d the bonus is charged to profit and loss to be divided among all the partners

6. *When a new partner is admitted to a partnership, or when an old partner dies or withdraws, it is most desirable*
   a to revalue the partners' assets
   b adjust the goodwill account
   c retain the existing values on the partnership books
   d record applicable bonuses

1 ________
2 ________
3 ________
4 ________
5 ________
6 ________

Scott and Taylor, partners, have capital investments of $10,000 and $5,000 respectively, and they share profits and losses equally. Prepare the journal entries to admit Phillips as a partner under each of the conditions indicated below (to check your answers, turn to page 49):

7. Phillips pays Scott $7,000 for 50% of Scott's interest.

8. Phillips receives a 1/3 interest by investing $12,-000. Goodwill is not to be recorded.

9. Phillips receives a 25% interest in a total capital of $18,000 by investing $3,000.

10. Phillips receives a 20% interest in a total capital of $25,000 by investing $5,000.

BASIC FACTS

Admission of a New Partner. The admission of a new partner requires the consent of all the partners. There are two methods by which an individual can acquire a partnership interest—by *purchase* from one of the old partners or by *investment* in the partnership.

Purchase of an Interest. When Jones purchases Smith's interest in the partnership of Smith and Brown, the transaction is between Jones and Smith. Accordingly, the partnership books reflect only the transfer of Smith's interest to Jones. The price paid and the terms of payment do not have any partnership effect and are not reflected on the books of account.

Investment in the Partnership. Unlike a purchase, an acquisition by investment increases the assets of the partnership. When the partner's capital account is to be credited for the exact amount of his investment, no problems arise.

In many situations the partnership will require that certain adjustments be made when recognizing an incoming partner's investment. This will happen when the partnership wants the incoming partner to pay for a portion of the goodwill of the firm or when the old partners feel that they are entitled to a bonus based on an unusually high earnings history. Similarly, the situation may be reversed and goodwill or a bonus may be recognized to the incoming partner.

Revaluation of Assets. When a new partner is admitted to a partnership or when an old partner dies or withdraws, it is desirable to revalue the partnership assets. This procedure will allow for a correct determination of the price to be paid for the transfer of partnership equity. Assets will be written up or down to bring the book figures into agreement with their fair market value. The net adjustment is always debited (or credited) to the partners' capital accounts in accordance with the predetermined profit and loss ratio.

(Continued on page 50)

ILLUSTRATIONS AND EXAMPLES

Admission of a New Partner

Purchase of an Interest

Smith, capital	10,000	
Jones, capital		10,000

To transfer Smith's interest to Jones (Jones paid Smith $12,000).

The fact that Jones paid a premium of $2,000 to Smith is not shown in the journal entry to record the transfer.

Investment in the Partnership

Simple Case—Credit for Exact Amount of Investment

Cash	10,000	
Jones, capital		10,000

To record admission of Jones to the partnership by investment of $10,000.

Complex Examples. Assume the following facts in the illustrations that follow: Smith and Jones are equal partners, each with a capital account of $40,000. Brown wishes to join the partnership and is willing to make an investment for his partnership interest.

(a) *Allowance of a bonus to the old partners.* Brown wishes to acquire a 20% interest in the partnership. The partnership requires an investment of $30,000. The following calculation is made to determine the amount of the credit to Brown's capital account:

Capital prior to investment	80,000
Investment	30,000
Capital after investment	110,000
Brown's 20% interest	22,000

The journal entry to record the investment is as follows:

Cash	30,000	
Brown, capital		22,000
Smith, capital		4,000
Jones, capital		4,000

To record admission of Brown with a 20% interest in profits and capital.

(b) *Recognition of goodwill to the old partners.* Instead of crediting the old partners with a bonus, an alternative method is to record the existence of goodwill on the books of the partnership. Assume that Brown is to invest $40,000 for a one-quarter interest in the partnership. Goodwill is to be recorded at a value based on Brown's $40,000 investment for a one-quarter interest.

Value of business as determined by Brown's investment (40,000 × 4)		160,000
Capital prior to investment	80,000	
Brown's investment	40,000	120,000
Goodwill to be recognized		40,000

(Continued on page 50)

EXPLANATIONS

1. *Partner X will receive* $25,000. Z's deficit balance, because of his personal bankruptcy, cannot be eliminated. It is to be treated as an additional loss to be shared by the remaining partners in their profit and loss ratio. X and Y each have equal interest in profits (40%), so each will absorb 50% of the $10,000 deficit. X will have to reduce his $30,000 credit balance by $5,000, leaving a balance of $25,000.

	PARTNER		
	X	Y	Z
Capital account prior to adjustment for Z's debit balance	$30,000	$20,000	($10,000)
Elimination of Z's debit balance	($ 5,000)	($ 5,000)	$10,000
Capital account prior to distribution of cash	$25,000	$15,000	0

2. *A new partner may be admitted to a partnership* with the consent of all the old partners.

3. *The following should be recorded on the partnership's books*: Richard's capital balance of $20,000 should be transferred to Marc. When a partner purchases an interest from another partner, the consideration paid does not have any effect on the partnership. It is a matter between the buyer and seller only. The capital account of the old partner becomes the property of the incoming partner and only the transfer need be recorded on the books.

4. *In the liquidation of a partnership, gains or losses resulting from the sale of operating assets should be divided among the partners* in the same ratio as operating income or loss. A gain or loss incurred in the liquidation of a partnership is divided among the partners in their profit and loss ratio. There is no distinction made between ordinary loss and losses incurred in winding up the partnership business.

5. *On the partnership books, if a bonus is given to a new partner to acknowledge the existence of certain special personal attributes* the old partners are charged for the bonus. The bonus to the new partner is a loss chargeable to the old partners in their profit and loss ratio.

6. *When a new partner is admitted to a partnership, or when an old partner dies or withdraws, it is most desirable* to revalue the partnership assets. Assets should be revalued when a partner is admitted or withdraws from the partnership. Failure to do so will mean that the new partner will participate in gains or losses attributable to the period prior to his admission.

7. *Phillips pays Scott $7,000 for 50% of Scott's interest.*

Scott, capital.	5,000	
Phillips, capital.		5,000

8. *Phillips receives a 1/3 interest by investing $12,000. Goodwill is not to be recorded.*

Cash	12,000	
Phillips, capital.		9,000
Scott, capital.		1,500
Taylor, capital		1,500

9. *Phillips receives a 25% interest in a total capital of $18,000 by investing $3,000.*

Cash	3,000	
Scott, capital.	750	
Taylor, capital	750	
Phillips, capital		4,500

10. *Phillips receives a 20% interest in a total capital of $25,000 by investing $5,000.*

Cash	5,000	
Goodwill	5,000	
Phillips, capital		5,000
Scott, capital.		2,500
Taylor, capital		2,500

Answers

c	1
b	2
c	3
b	4
c	5
a	6

Withdrawal of a Partner. When a partner withdraws from a partnership, he may receive cash or other assets from either the remaining partner(s) or from the partnership. If the transaction is between the partners, the entry is similar to that for the purchase of an interest. The partnership books merely record the transfer of the interest, at the book value. If the partnership uses its own assets to accomplish the retirement, the entry may require the recognition of a bonus (to the retiring partner or to the remaining partners) or the revaluation of partnership assets. The previous discussion on investment in a partnership applies to partnership withdrawals. Increases or decreases resulting from asset revaluation are divided among all the partners in their profit and loss ratio; bonuses also are debited or credited to the remaining partners in the profit and loss ratio.

Liquidation of a Partnership. When a partnership ceases to carry on any business and sells off all of its assets, it is said to be in a state of liquidation. The sale of the operating assets usually will result in a gain or loss to the partnership since the fair market value of the assets sold will rarely be identical with their book value. The gain or loss will be divided among the partners in the same ratio as operating income or losses. Before any cash is distributed to the partners, the creditors must be paid in full.

Partner with Debit Balance. It is possible that after being charged with his share of the loss from the sale of the partnership assets a partner will have a debit balance in his capital account. If this occurs, the partner should pay into the partnership sufficient cash to bring his account to a zero balance. If he is unable to do so, the debit balance is treated as an additional loss to be absorbed by the remaining partners in their profit and loss ratio. Each partner will receive a cash liquidating distribution equal to his capital account balance, less his share of the debit balance.

The entries required are:

(1) Goodwill	40,000	
Smith, capital		20,000
Jones, capital		20,000

To record goodwill based on Brown's investment, shared by original partners in their profit and loss ratio.

(2) Cash	40,000	
Brown, capital		40,000

To record Brown's investment of $40,000 for a 25% interest in capital and profits.

(c) *Recognition of goodwill to incoming partner.* Brown is willing to contribute the operating assets of an existing business that he owns for a one-third interest in the partnership. Because of the exceptional earning power of the business, the partners are willing to recognize the existence of goodwill to Brown in the amount of $15,000. The value of the tangible assets being contributed is $25,000. The journal entry is as follows:

Goodwill	15,000	
Various assets	25,000	
Brown, capital		40,000

To record admission of Brown to a one-third interest in the partnership upon contribution of goodwill and tangible assets.

(d) *Recognition of bonus to new partner.* In recognizing a bonus to the incoming partner, the partnership acknowledges the existence of certain special attributes of the new partner. If Brown contributes $28,000 for a one-third interest in the partnership, a bonus of $8,000 is being granted to him. The computation of the bonus and the journal entries to record the transactions are as follows:

Capital prior to investment	80,000
Brown's investment	28,000
Total capital	108,000
Brown's capital credit (1/3 of 108,000)	36,000
Brown's cash contribution	28,000
Bonus allowed to Brown	8,000

Smith, capital	4,000	
Jones, capital	4,000	
Brown, capital		8,000

To charge Smith and Jones for bonus allowed upon Brown's admission to a one-third interest in the partnership.

Cash	28,000	
Brown, capital		28,000

To record Brown's cash contribution to partnership upon his admission to a one-third interest in the partnership.

Withdrawal of a Partner.

Brown withdraws from a partnership at a time when his capital account shows a $40,000 credit balance. He receives $50,000 for his interest. If the remaining partners are charged for the differential, the following entry would be made:

Brown, capital	40,000	
Smith, capital	5,000	
Jones, capital	5,000	
Cash		50,000

To record payment of $50,000 to Brown upon complete liquidation of his one-third interest at $10,000 over his capital account balance.

13 CORPORATIONS I
CHARACTERISTICS & CAPITAL STOCK

SELF-TEST

DIRECTIONS: Write your answers (T or F) in the numbered lines to the right. To check your answers, turn to page **53**.

1. The par value of stock is closely related to the stock's fair market value.
2. Common stock carries greater risks of ownership than preferred stock.
3. Preferred stockholders control the operations of a corporation through the election of the members of the board of directors.
4. Where only one class of stock exists, it is termed common stock.
5. In the liquidation of a corporation, creditors' claims are superior to the interest of both common and preferred stockholders.
6. Preferred stockholders are guaranteed dividends at a fixed annual rate.
7. Convertible preferred stock can be redeemed at a fixed price.
8. The "pre-emptive right" grants shareholders the right to receive dividends in excess of the fixed dividend rate.
9. In the case of cumulative preferred stock, if a dividend has been omitted in a previous year the amount in arrears will have to be made up in subsequent years before any distributions to common stock.
10. The owners of common stock have the right to contract for the corporation.
11. Participating preferred shares receive dividends at a fixed rate.

1 ______

2 ______

3 ______

4 ______

5 ______

6 ______

7 ______

8 ______

9 ______

10 ______

11 ______

BASIC FACTS

Characteristics of the Corporation. The U. S. Supreme Court has defined a corporation to be "an artificial being, invisible, intangible, and existing only in contemplation of law." A corporation's existence is established by the laws of the state in which it is incorporated. It is a legal entity separate from its owners. It can be sued in its own name and pays income taxes on its earnings. There are several basic characteristics that distinguish the corporation from the partnership or sole proprietorship. They are: (1) limited liability to stockholders, usually limited to the amount invested in the corporation; (2) transferability of units of ownership, known as shares of stock; (3) perpetual life.

Capital Stock. The ownership of a corporation is evidenced by units known as shares of stock. Stock may be either *par value* stock or *no par value* stock. If a stock has a par value, each share has been given a face value which is printed on the stock certificate. The par value is an arbitrarily determined amount and bears no relationship to the actual fair market value of the shares. If the shares are not given a designated par value, the stock is termed no-par stock. Even though the stock has no face value, many states require that the stock be assigned a *stated value.* This stated value is similar to par value in that it bears no relationship to either fair market value or book value.

The two major classes of stock are:

Common Stock grants to the owner all rights normally accompanying ownership. This includes the right to vote, the right to share in earnings (through the receipt of dividends), the pre-emptive right to maintain proportional ownership, and the right to share upon liquidation. If a corporation has only one class of stock, it will be termed common stock. Where a second or preferred class of stock exists, certain rights of the common shareholders will be subordinated, as discussed below.

Preferred Stock was developed to remove some of the risks of ownership interest in common stock. To compensate for the greater security, the right to vote is usually not conferred on the preferred

(*Continued on page 54*)

ILLUSTRATIONS AND EXAMPLES

Common Stock and Preferred Stock

Dividend Distributions

1. *Simple Case.* The capital section of the Richards Corp. appears below:

Preferred 5% stock, non-participating, non-cumulative, $100 par	$ 500,000
Common stock, $10 par	1,000,000
Retained earnings	2,500,000
	$4,000,000

Semi-annual dividend distribution includes a $2.00 per share common stock dividend. The dividends would be distributed:

Preferred stock (2½% × $500,000)	$ 12,500
Common stock ($2.00 × 100,000 shares)	200,000
	$212,500

(*Continued on page 54*)

EXPLANATIONS

1. *The par value of stock is* not *closely related to the stock's market value,* but is merely the face amount of the certificate. It is an arbitrarily determined figure and only coincidentally has any relationship to the fair market value.

2. *Common stock carries greater risks of ownership than preferred stock.* The preferences attaching to preferred shares minimize the risks inherent in common stock ownership.

3. *Preferred stockholders do* not *control the operations of a corporation through the election of the members of the board of directors.* Preferred shareholders do not elect the members of the board of directors, this is done by the common stockholders.

4. *Where only one class of stock exists, it is termed common stock*, and each share has equal rights.

5. *In the liquidation of a corporation, creditors' claims are superior to the interest of both common and preferred stockholders.* Most preferred stocks are entitled to payment of a stated value before payment is made to the common shareholders.

6. *Preferred stockholders are* not *guaranteed dividends at a fixed annual rate*; however, the preferred stock is usually entitled to receive a stated dividend before any distributions are made on the common shares.

7. *Convertible preferred stock can* not *be redeemed at a fixed price.* Callable preferred stock, not convertible preferred, is redeemable at a fixed rate. Convertible preferred is exchangeable for common shares at a fixed rate at the option of the stockholder.

8. *The "pre-emptive right" does* not *grant shareholders the right to receive dividends in excess of the fixed dividend rate,* nor does it give any rights relating to dividends. The pre-emptive right is a privilege granted to shareholders to enable them to retain their proportionate share in the equity of the corporation. This is done by allowing each stockholder to subscribe proportionally to any new stock issued.

9. *In the case of cumulative preferred stock, if a dividend has been omitted in a previous year the amount in arrears will have to be made up in subsequent years before any distributions to common stock.* Where a dividend has been omitted on cumulative preferred stock, it will have to be made up before any distributions can be paid to the common shareholders.

10. *The owners of common stock do* not *have the right to contract for the corporation.* The owner of common stock is not entitled to transact any business on behalf of the corporation. This would preclude the right to contract on behalf of the corporation.

11. *Participating preferred shares do* not *receive dividends at a fixed rate.* Participating preferred shares may receive dividends in excess of the fixed rate. After the fixed rate is paid to both preferred and common, the participating preferred shares usually share equally with the common stock in any additional dividend paid.

Answers

F	1
T	2
F	3
T	4
T	5
F	6
F	7
F	8
T	9
F	10
F	11

shareholder. The preferences to be granted the preferred shareholder are many and varied. Several of the more common include: the right to receive a fixed rate of dividend *before* any dividend is paid to the common shareholder, which is the most common privilege attaching to preferred stock.

Participating Preferred. The preferred shareholders have the right to receive dividends in excess of the fixed dividend rate. If the preferred stock is limited to the fixed rate, then the stock is said to be *non-participating.*

Cumulative or *Non-cumulative Preferred.* Dividends are declared at the discretion of the board of directors and there is no guarantee that an annual distribution will be paid. In order to give additional security to the preferred stockholders, the stock may have a *cumulative* feature. Then, in those cases where a dividend is omitted in a particular year or years, the amount in arrears will have to be made up in subsequent years (dividends in arrears). The common shareholders cannot receive any dividend until all arrearage has been paid to the preferred shareholders. If the preferred stock is *non-cumulative,* then any omitted dividends need not be made up.

Convertible Preferred. This stock grants to the owners the right to convert the stock into another form of security. Usually, the conversion privilege grants the right to convert the preferred stock into common stock of the company at a fixed rate. The right to convert is almost always at the option of the stockholder, rather than of the corporation.

Preference as to Assets. In case of liquidation of the corporation, the preferred shareholders will receive a distribution from the corporation prior to the common shareholders. Payment must still be subordinated to the claims of the creditors.

Certain Unfavorable Aspects of Preferred Stock. In most situations the preferred stock has either no voting rights or limited voting rights. The stock may also be *callable,* which means that at the option of the issuing corporation, the preferred shares are called for redemption at a stipulated price.

2. *Participating Preferred.* The capital section of Fryer Inc. appears below:

Preferred 6% stock, fully participating, non-cumulative, $100 par	$1,000,000
Common stock, $50 par	2,500,000
Retained earnings	3,000,000
	$6,500,000

If the total dividends for the year amounted to $540,000 they would be distributed as follows:

(a) Preferred stock receives the normal dividends first: $6 × 10,000 shares	$ 60,000
(b) Common stock receives a comparable dividend: $6 × 50,000 shares	300,000
(c) Remaining amount is to be distributed equally per share	180,000
	$540,000

	On Preferred Shares (10,000 shares)	On Common Shares (50,000 shares)	Total
Regular dividend	$60,000		$60,000
Comparable dividend		$300,000	300,000
Remaining amount	30,000	150,000	180,000
	$90,000	$450,000	$540,000
	($9 per share)	($9 per share)	

3. *Cumulative Preferred–Dividend in Arrears.* The capital section of the Marc Corporation appears below:

Preferred stock 4%, non-participating, cumulative (dividend in arrears for 2 years), $100 par	$ 300,000
Common stock, $5 par	1,000,000
Retained earnings	60,000
	$1,360,000

The board of directors has declared a total dividend distribution for the year of $40,000. This would be distributed in the following manner:

(a) Preferred stock receives the dividends in arrears: $4 × 3,000 shares = $12,000 × 2 years	$24,000
(b) Preferred stock receives the current year dividend	12,000
Total distributed to preferred	36,000
(c) Balance remaining is distributed to common	4,000
	$40,000

14 CORPORATIONS II
INVESTMENTS & TREASURY STOCK

SELF-TEST

DIRECTIONS: For questions 1–5, write your answers (a, b, c, or d) on the numbered lines to the right. To check your answers, turn to page 57.

1 ______

2 ______

3 ______

4 ______

5 ______

1. *If stock is sold by the issuing corporation at a price above par value*
   a the proceeds are credited to premium on capital stock
   b the excess over par is credited to premium on capital stock
   c the proceeds are credited to capital stock
   d the excess over par is credited to capital stock

2. *Outstanding shares refers to*
   a the maximum number of shares that can be issued
   b shares which have at one time been sold by the corporation
   c shares in the hands of stockholders
   d shares once issued by the corporation which have been subsequently reacquired

3. *Treasury stock held by the issuing corporation and not cancelled*
   a may be sold at any price
   b is entitled to receive dividends
   c is eligible to subscribe to new shares (preemptive right)
   d may be sold only at par value or above

4. *Balance sheet presentation of treasury stock*
   a is most frequently an asset
   b is most frequently a deduction from contributed capital and retained earnings
   c is most frequently between the liability and stockholders' equity sections
   d is most frequently a current liability

5. *Subscriptions receivable would normally be shown on the balance sheet as*
   a a current asset
   b an other asset
   c a deduction from capital stock
   d a deduction from contributed capital and retained earnings

6. *From the following information prepare journal entries to record the transactions. Prepare the stockholders' equity section of the corporation balance sheet at June 30, 19___:*

   X Corporation has 250,000 shares of $5 par value common stock authorized. 100,000 shares were issued at $6.50 per share. Preferred 5% capital stock, authorized 1000 shares of $100 par value, was completely issued at $110. Subsequently, the corporation reacquired 5000 shares of common stock at a cost of $7.50 per share. Retained earnings at the balance sheet date amounted to $175,000.

BASIC FACTS

Recording the Stockholders' Investment. The certificate of incorporation indicates the maximum number of shares of each class of capital stock that can be issued. The number is termed the *authorized* shares. It is desirable that the corporation authorize sufficient shares to provide for possible additional financing at a future date. If the authorized shares prove to be insufficient for the corporation's business, an amendment to the certificate of incorporation can be filed, to increase the authorized shares.

The *authorized* shares may be either *issued* or *unissued.* Issued shares are those which have at one time been sold by the corporation. The unissued shares are those which have not been sold.

The issued shares may be *outstanding* or *treasury* shares. Outstanding shares are those in the hands of stockholders, while treasury stock are shares once issued by the corporation which have been subsequently reacquired.

The authorized shares of stock are not recorded by formal journal entries. A memorandum is made in the general journal, indicating the number of authorized shares of each class of capital stock.

Issuance of Par-Value Stock

Sold at Par. The capital stock account is credited for the number of shares issued multiplied by the par value.

Sold at Price above Par. In many instances the price paid to the issuing corporation is above the par value. The capital stock accounts are reflected at par value, regardless of the price paid to the corporation. Excess over par (premium) is credited to a capital account, entitled *premium on capital stock* or *paid-in capital in excess of par value.*

Sold at price below Par. It is possible that the stock be issued at a price below par (discount). The capital stock account is credited at the par value and the deficiency is debited to an account *discount on capital stock.* Many states prohibit the issuance of stock at less than par, and it is usual for the par value to be reduced so that such a situation would not arise. It must be recognized that once the stock has been issued it may be traded at any price.

Issuance of No-Par and Stated Value Stock. Because of various abuses associated with the concept of par value, most states permit the issuance of capital stock without a par value. The advantages of no-par include: (a) the potential liability to stockholders above their investment where stock has been issued at a discount is avoided; (b) the printed par value often led investors to form unfounded conclusions as to the worth of the stock; (c) in the case where assets other than cash are accepted for payment, a fair valuation is encouraged.

In several states a stated or assigned value by the board of directors may be given for each share.

Underwriting Costs of Stock Issues. Where the issue of capital stock is substantial in amount, the corporation uses an investment banking firm to underwrite and market the securities. The underwriter receives a fee or purchases the securities for later sale to the investing public. In either case the issuing corporation enters in its books only the net amount received.

(*Continued on page 58*)

ILLUSTRATIONS AND EXAMPLES

Issuance of Par-Value Stock

Sold at Par. If the stock is sold for cash at the par value, the following entry is made:

Cash	10,000	
Common stock		10,000

To record the issuance of 1,000 shares of common stock at a par value of $10 per share.

Sold at Price Above Par. If in the foregoing illustration the price paid had been $15 a share, the following entry would have been made:

Cash	15,000	
Common stock		10,000
Premium on common stock		5,000

No-Par and Stated Value.

No-par

Cash	13,000	
Common stock		13,000

To record issuance of 1,000 shares of no-par common stock for $13,000.

Stated value

Cash	13,000	
Common stock		10,000
Paid-in capital in excess of stated value		3,000

To record issuance of 1000 shares of common stock, stated value $10 per share.

(*Continued on page 58*)

EXPLANATIONS

1. *If stock is sold by the issuing corporation at a price above par value,* the excess over par is credited to premium on capital stock. Thus, the premium is part of the shareholders' investment and is paid-in or contributed capital. The excess amount is credited to a separate account, premium on capital stock.

2. *Outstanding shares refers to* shares in the hands of stockholders. The corporation's charter establishes the maximum number of shares that may be issued. This amount is known as the authorized shares. The authorized shares may be issued or unissued. Issued shares in the hands of outsiders are known as outstanding shares. Issued shares reacquired and still held but not cancelled by the corporation are treasury shares.

3. *Treasury stock held by the issuing corporation and not cancelled* may be sold at any price. Treasury shares, since they have been previously issued, may be sold below par value. The purchasing shareholder will not be liable to creditors for the amount equal to the discount on the stock.

4. *Balance sheet presentation of treasury stock* is most frequently a deduction from contributed capital and retained earnings. When treasury stock is purchased the corporation, in a sense, is contracting its stockholders' equity. Rights of ownership such as the right to vote and receive dividends do not accrue to treasury shares. Therefore, it is not appropriate to consider them assets.

5. *Subscriptions receivable would normally be shown on the balance sheet as* a current asset since this represents the amount due from shareholders on their agreements to purchase capital stock from the corporation. Generally, such amounts would be due within one year and should be shown as a current asset.

Answers

b	1
c	2
a	3
b	4
a	5

6.

Cash	650,000	
Common stock		500,000
Premium on common stock		150,000

To record issuance of 100,000 shares of common stock, par value $5.00 for $6.50.

Cash	110,000	
Preferred stock		100,000
Premium on preferred stock		10,000

To record issuance of 1000 shares of $100 par value preferred stock at $110 per share.

Treasury stock–common	37,500	
Cash		37,500

To record purchase of 5000 shares of common stock at $7.50 per share.

X Corporation
Stockholders' Equity Section
June 30, 19__

Capital Stock:		
Preferred 5% capital stock, par value $100 authorized, issued and outstanding 1000 shares		$100,000
Common stock, $5 par value, authorized 250,000 shares; issued 100,000 shares, of which 5000 are held in treasury		500,000
Additional paid-in capital:		
Premium on preferred stock	10,000	
Premium on common stock	150,000	160,000
Retained earnings		175,000
		$935,000
Deduct: Common stock held in treasury, 5000 shares at cost		37,500
Stockholders' equity		$897,500

Subscriptions to Capital Stock. In the preceding discussion the corporation had issued the stock based on the receipt of cash (or other assets). It is common practice that before the actual receipt of assets the future stockholders will agree to subscribe to the shares. The subscription agreement is binding and, therefore, an asset exists on the corporation's books. The actual shares are not issued until full payment has been made.

Treasury Stock. A corporation may occasionally reacquire its own issued capital stock. The term "treasury stock" denotes such shares when in the hands of the issuing corporation and not cancelled. Such shares are not entitled to the rights to receive dividends, to vote, or to subscribe to new shares (pre-emptive right).

Recording Purchases and Sales. Usually the purchase of treasury stock is recorded at cost by debiting an account entitled *treasury stock.* The entry on the books is recorded at the cost to the corporation, regardless of the existence of a par or stated value or the price at which the shares were originally issued.

When the treasury shares are re-sold, a credit is made to the treasury stock account for the cash price paid for the shares. Any profit or loss on the sale is recorded as a debit or credit to an account called *paid in capital from sale of treasury stock;* this is not an income account, but a capital account.

Donated Treasury Stock. In certain instances stockholders may donate shares of capital stock to the corporation. Since there is no change in the total assets or stockholders' equity, only a memorandum is required at the time of donation. When the shares are sold by the corporation, the proceeds would be credited to a paid-in capital account.

Balance Sheet Presentation. There are several acceptable methods of balance sheet presentation of treasury stock. It is most frequently shown as a deduction from the total of contributed capital and retained earnings. Treasury stock is not an asset of the corporation and only in unusual situations should it be shown on the asset side of the balance sheet.

Subscriptions to Capital Stock

Cash	6,000	
Subscriptions receivable	24,000	
Common stock subscribed		20,000
Premium on common stock		10,000

Received subscriptions for 2,000 shares of $10 par value common stock at $15 per share, with a down payment of 20%.

Cash	12,000	
Subscriptions receivable		12,000

To record receipt of remaining 80% due on 1,000 shares previously subscribed.

Common stock subscribed	10,000	
Common stock		10,000

Issued certificates for 1,000 shares of common stock.

For balance sheet purposes, the subscriptions receivable would appear as a current asset and the common stock subscribed as part of the paid-in capital.

Treasury Stock

Recording Purchases of Treasury Stock:

Treasury stock	2,500	
Cash		2,500

Purchased 100 shares of $10 par common stock (treasury) at $25 per share.

Recording Sales of Treasury Stock:

Cash	1,500	
Treasury stock		1,250
Paid-in capital from sale of treasury stock		250

Sold 50 shares of the $10 par common stock (treasury) at $30 per share, acquired at a cost of $25 per share.

15 CORPORATIONS III
RETAINED EARNINGS, DIVIDENDS

SELF-TEST

DIRECTIONS: For questions 1–8, write your answers (T or F) on the numbered lines to the right. To check your answers, turn to page **61**.

1. Dividends can legally be paid out of current or accumulated earnings.
2. Dividends in arrears on cumulative preferred stock should be reflected in the balance sheet as a current liability.
3. Stock split-ups are effected to reduce the unit selling price of shares.
4. Stock dividends and stock split-ups are recorded in the capital section in the identical manner.
5. When the number of shares issued is greater than 50% of the previously outstanding shares, a stock split-up has been effected, rather than a stock dividend.
6. Dividends may take the form of cash, property, or stock of the issuing corporation.
7. The board of directors must declare some kind of dividend if there is any accumulated earnings.
8. An appropriation of retained earnings may not be discretionary on the part of the corporation.

1 ________
2 ________
3 ________
4 ________
5 ________
6 ________
7 ________
8 ________

The following is the stockholders' equity section as it appears on a corporation's balance sheet.

Alison Corporation
Stockholders' Equity
December 31, 19__

Preferred stock–6% cumulative, non participating $100 par value; 2,000 shares authorized and outstanding		$ 200,000
Common stock $25 par value; 60,000 shares authorized and outstanding		1,500,000
Premium on common stock		100,000
Retained earnings		
Appropriated for plant expansion	$ 150,000	
Appropriated for bonded indebtedness	500,000	
Appropriated for contingencies	250,000	
Unappropriated	2,100,000	3,000,000
Total stockholders' equity		$4,800,000

Additional facts:

(A) There are no dividends in arrears on the preferred stock.
(B) In the event of liquidation, the preferred shares are entitled only to par plus unpaid cumulative dividends.
(C) The bond indenture requires annual appropriations of retained earnings over the life of the bonds.

9. What is the total amount of permanent capital?
10. What is the book value per share of preferred stock?
11. What is the total amount of the discretionary appropriations to retained earnings?
12. What is the book value per share of common stock?

To check your answers, turn to page **61**.

BASIC FACTS

Distinction Between Paid-in Capital and Retained Earnings. The net worth section of the corporate balance sheet shows the sources of corporate capital. *Contributed capital* and *income* (*undistributed profits*) are the two principal sources. There is a further breakdown of contributed capital, based on the distinction between (1) capital contributed for shares to the extent of their par or stated value; (2) amounts contributed for shares in excess of such par or stated value; and (3) amounts received other than for shares.

"*Retained earnings*" has received general acceptance as the terminology to describe undistributed profits; there is little standardization in accounting terminology to indicate contributed capital. The term "*paid-in capital*" is often used as a generic title to include all items of contributed capital other than amounts paid for stock to the extent of par or stated value.

Major sources of paid-in capital include: (1) issuance of par value stock for amounts in excess of par value; (2) issuance of stated value stock for amounts in excess of stated value; (3) the excess above cost received from the sale of treasury stock; (4) the purchase and subsequent retirement of capital stock of the corporation at a cost less than the issue price; and (5) gifts of property to the corporation.

Dividends. A dividend represents a pro-rata distribution of assets by a corporation to its shareholders. The dividend is usually paid in cash but may also be in the form of property or stock of the issuing company. Dividends usually are paid from either current or accumulated earnings. Many states permit dividends to be paid from paid-in capital. The effect of this is to give back to the stockholders a portion of their investment. Dividends are declared by formal action of the board of directors and, in the case of cash dividends, are recorded as a current liability on the date of declaration. The directors are *not required* to declare either preferred or common stock dividends. In the case of cumulative preferred stock, the amount of dividends in arrears is shown as a footnote to the financial statements or by parenthetic notation or by an appropriation of retained earnings.

Recording Cash Dividends. At the date of declaration, and entry is made debiting the "Dividends Paid" account. This account would be closed to retained earnings.

Recording Stock Dividends. Stock dividends usually take the form of additional shares of common stock of the corporation being issued to present holders of common stock. There is no distribution of cash or other assets and, therefore, no change in total assets or stockholders' equity results from the stock dividend. The only effect is to "capitalize" retained earnings by a transfer into capital stock and paid-in capital. The transfer from retained earnings is made, using the fair market value of the shares on the date of declaration.

The receipt of the stock dividend does not represent income to the shareholders. The stock dividend payable account is not a liability to the corporation and on a balance sheet would be shown in the stockholders' equity section immediately below common stock.

(*Continued on page 62*)

ILLUSTRATIONS AND EXAMPLES

Recording Cash Dividends

Retained earnings (or Dividends Paid on Common Stock)	5,000	
Dividends Payable		5,000

To record the declaration of the quarterly dividend of $.50 on 10,000 shares of $1 par common stock.

The cash payment is recorded:

Dividends payable	5,000	
Cash		5,000

Recording Stock Dividends.

At the date of declaration the following entry is made:

Retained Earnings	12,500	
Stock Dividends Payable (Stock Dividend Distributable)		5,000
Paid-in Capital from Stock Dividends		7,500

To record the declaration of a 5% stock dividend on $10 par value common stock (outstanding shares 10,000); the fair market value of the stock is $25 per share.

At the date of issuance of the shares the following entry would be made:

Stock Dividends Payable (Stock Dividend Distributable)	5,000	
Common Stock		5,000

(*Continued on page 62*)

EXPLANATIONS

1. *Dividends can legally be paid out of current or accumulated earnings*, since they are distributions of earnings. Legally, the entire amount of accumulated earnings is available for distribution. As a practical matter, it is very rare for directors to declare a dividend equal to 100% of earnings.

2. *Dividends in arrears on cumulative preferred stock should* not *be reflected in the balance sheet as a current liability*. A dividend is not a liability until it has been declared by the board of directors and notice has been given to the shareholders. Dividends in arrears on cumulative preferred stock must be paid before any dividends can be paid on common shares. Until a dividend is declared, no liability exists for its payment.

3. *Stock split-ups are effected to reduce the unit selling price of shares*. A price reduction should improve the marketability of the shares and establish a wider shareholder base.

4. *Stock dividends and stock split-ups are* not *recorded identically in the capital section*. In recording a stock dividend, the fair market value of the shares issued is transferred from retained earnings to the capital stock and paid-in capital accounts. A stock split-up does not require the transfer from retained earnings to the permanent capital accounts.

5. *When the number of shares issued is greater than 50% of the previously outstanding shares, a stock split-up has been effected, rather than a stock dividend*. There is no hard and fast rule as to when a distribution should be classified as a stock dividend or a stock split. However, it is generally acknowledged that a stock dividend involves the issuance of not more than 25% of the number of previously outstanding shares. When the shares issued is greater than 25% of the previously outstanding shares, a stock split-up is indicated.

6. *Dividends may take the form of cash, property, or stock of the issuing corporation*. When cash is needed in the business, dividends are very often paid in stock of the issuing corporation. Corporations of medium or large size find it impractical to declare dividends in property.

7. *The board of directors does* not *have to declare some kind of dividend if there is any accumulated earnings*. Dividends are declared solely at the discretion of the board of directors. Even though the corporation has earnings, there is no requirement that any portion of these earnings be distributed to the shareholders.

8. *An appropriation of retained earnings may not be discretionary on the part of the corporation*. An appropriation of retained earnings is done to make clear to readers of the balance sheet that the appropriated portion is not available for the payment of dividends. It is not always discretionary; some appropriations are contractual. Often the terms of the bond indenture will require a restriction on the payment of dividends until the debt is repaid.

9. *The total amount of permanent capital is* \$1,800,000. The permanent capital is the amount paid by the shareholders upon issuance of stock. It includes premium paid for shares issued above par or stated value. In the illustration, the permanent capital includes \$200,000 of preferred stock, \$1,500,000 of common stock, and the \$100,000 premium paid on common stock.

10. *The book value per share of preferred stock is* \$100. On liquidation, the preferred stock is entitled to par value plus any cumulative dividends. Since there were no dividends in arrears, the preferred stock is only entitled to par value of \$100, or \$200,000 on the shares outstanding.

11. *The total amount of the discretionary appropriations to retained earnings is* \$400,000. The appropriation for bonded indebtedness is required under the terms of the bond indenture and is therefore contractual, not discretionary. The discretionary appropriations are for contingencies and plant expansion.

12. *The book value per share of common stock is* \$76.67.

Total stockholders' equity	\$4,800,000
Portion applicable to preferred stock	200,000
Remainder applicable to common stock . .	\$4,600,000

Book value per share = \$4,600,000 ÷ 60,000 = \$76.67.

Answers

T	1
F	2
T	3
F	4
T	5
T	6
F	7
T	8

Stock Dividend vs. Stock Split-up. A stock split-up is effected by a reduction of the par or stated value of a corporation's common stock and the issuance of a proportionate number of additional shares. The difference between a stock dividend and a stock split is based on the intention of the board of directors in making the distribution. The primary purpose of a stock split is to reduce the unit selling price of the shares. It is used by corporations whose shares are publicly held and regularly traded. The purpose of a stock dividend is to make a distribution of earnings. It is generally accepted that where the number of shares issued is less than 20% or 25% of the number of previously outstanding shares, a stock dividend has been effectuated. Where the number of shares is greater than 20% or 25%, there is a reasonable expectation of a material reduction in the unit selling price of a share, which indicates a stock split-up.

Appropriations of Retained Earnings. There are many situations when the directors of a corporation will set apart a portion of the retained earnings for a specific purpose or use. Such an appropriation may be made voluntarily, but most often it is done to comply with the requirements of a contract or law. Its purpose is to assure that the corporation's capital will not be impaired by restricting the amount of retained earnings available for dividends.

Book Value of Capital Stock. The book value of a share of stock bears no relationship to its fair market value. It is an arithmetic value arrived at by dividing the stockholders' equity by the number of shares outstanding. The book value of a share of stock has limited significance as a guide to the reasonableness of the market price of a stock. One must be cautioned against placing too much reliance on book value as a measure of market value. The worth of a business to its owners is determined by corporate earnings. The price-earnings ratio will continue to exercise far greater influence on market value than a price-equity ratio.

Other Values

Redemption Value (call price). This term is applicable to preferred stock. The call price to be paid by the issuing corporation is usually set at an amount slightly in excess of par value.

Market Value. This is the price at which a share of stock can be currently purchased or sold.

Stock Split-up

A corporation has 50,000 shares of $10 par value common stock outstanding. The corporation reduces the par value to $5 per share and issues to the shareholders an additional 50,000 shares of stock. Each stockholder now owns two shares for each one he held prior to the split. There are no changes in the dollar amount of any balance sheet accounts; therefore, there is no journal entry necessary to record the split-up.

Recording Appropriations of Retained Earnings

Retained Earnings	25,000	
Retained Earnings Appropriated for Treasury Stock		25,000

To record reduction of retained earnings by $25,000, the amount paid on the acquisition of 1000 shares of treasury stock.

Book Value of Capital Stock

Common Stock, 1000 shares no par value	$20,000
Paid-in Capital in excess of stated value	12,500
Retained Earnings	50,000
Total Stockholders' Equity	$82,500

The book value per share is $82.50 ($82,500 ÷ 1000).

Liquidating Value. This is an estimate of the amount that each share will receive if the corporation were to (1) discontinue business; (2) pay off all creditors; (3) convert the remaining assets to cash; and (4) distribute the cash pro-rata to the shareholders.

16 LIABILITIES

SELF-TEST

DIRECTIONS: For questions 1-9, indicate the correct balance sheet treatment by writing a, b, or c on the numbered lines to the right. To check your answers, turn to page 65.

a Current Liability Section

b Long-Term Liability Section

c Footnote

1. Notes receivable discounted. 1 ________
2. Accounts payable for goods in transit. 2 ________
3. Pending lawsuit. 3 ________
4. Employees' taxes withheld. 4 ________
5. Temporary borrowings from affiliates. 5 ________
6. Maturing bonds which are to be refunded. 6 ________
7. Current sinking fund installment on long-term mortgage bonds. 7 ________
8. Firm commitment for purchase of materials. 8 ________
9. Accrued liabilities. 9 ________
10. Prepare journal entries to record the following set of facts for the period from March 1, 1967 to January 15, 1968. Adjusting and closing entries are made at year-end (December 31).

    On January 1, 1967, the shareholders of XYZ Corporation authorized the issuance of $2,000,000 of 6%, 10-year debenture bonds. The bonds were to be registered and pay interest on January 1 and July 1. On March 1, 1967 $1,000,000 par value of the bonds were issued at 101½ plus accrued interest. On July 1, 1967 an additional $800,000 par value of the bonds were issued at 102. On January 1, 1968 the company purchased $300,000 of bonds on the open market at 101 plus accrued interest. All required interest payments were made by the corporation.

To check your answer, turn to page 65.

BASIC FACTS

Liabilities represent debts or obligations of an entity, to be settled at a future date by the disbursement of an asset (most often cash) or by the rendering of services to the creditor. There are two main classes, *current liabilities* and *long-term liabilities*. Current liabilities are those which are due within the operating cycle of the business or one year, whichever period is longer. Notes payable, accounts payable, and accrued expenses, are examples.

Debt vs. Equity Financing. A business has several alternatives in financing, any of which may be used to varying degrees. Short-term requirements may be met by borrowing from banks or through the use of trade credit. For long-term financing a corporation may resort to borrowing basis through the sale of bonds.

In evaluating debt financing by the use of bonds and equity financing by issuance of capital stock, several factors must be considered:

1. Bonds represent a definite commitment on the part of the issuer to pay interest and principal.
2. Interest payments are an expense of operations and are deductible for income tax purposes. Dividends are a distribution of income and are not tax deductible.
3. Certain types of investors, such as financial institutions and charitable organizations, are restricted as to the amount and type of investments they can make in corporate stocks.

Nature of Bonds. Bonds are sold in various face or principal amounts, but the most common denomination is $1,000. Interest payments are usually made on a semi-annual basis.

Journalizing the Issuance of Bonds. The approval by the stockholders of the details of the proposed bond issue is usually required. No formal journal entry is required to record the authorization of the bond issue. A liability does not exist until bonds are actually issued and a debtor-creditor relationship has been established. At that time a *bonds payable* (liability) account is recorded on the books. The bonds may be sold at par, a discount from par, or at a premium over par.

Issuance between Interest Dates. The issuing corporation pays interest for a full period to the holder of a bond on the last day of the interest period. This would create inequities in the many instances where bonds are bought and sold during an interest period. To correct this

(*Continued on page 66*)

ILLUSTRATIONS AND EXAMPLES

Journalizing the Issuance of Bonds

Bonds Sold at Par. On January 1, 1968 $3,000,000 of 10 year, 6% bonds (interest payable January 1 and July 1) were sold at "100," the face value. The following entry is made:

Cash	3,000,000	
Bonds payable		3,000,000

Bonds Sold at a Discount. If the contract rate of interest is less than the prevailing market rate for the particular grade of bonds, the bonds must be sold on a discount basis. The discount will be sufficient to create an effective interest rate equal to the current market rate. The following entry illustrates the issuance of a $3,000,000 bond issue at "96":

Cash	2,880,000	
Discount on bonds payable	120,000	
Bonds payable		3,000,000

The four point discount (100 – 96), when applied to the $3,000,000 of bonds issued, results in a $120,000 deferred charge, called discount on bonds payable. This sum will be charged against revenues as additional interest over the term of the bonds.

Bonds Sold at a Premium. As contrasted to the bond discount situation, the contract rate may be greater than the prevailing market rate. The bonds are then issued at a premium, a price greater than the face value. If the preceding bond issue was sold at 102, the following entry is made:

Cash	3,060,000	
Bonds payable		3,000,000
Premium on bonds payable		60,000

Issuance Between Interest Dates. Assume that a $3,000,000, 6% bond issue with a ten year term, is sold on February 1 at 103. Interest is paid semi-annually on January 1 and July 1. The following journal entry is made to record the sale:

Feb. 1	Cash	3,105,000	
	Bonds payable		3,000,000
	Premium on bonds payable		90,000
	Interest expense (or accrued bond interest)		15,000

On July 1st the bondholders will receive interest for an entire semi-annual period, even though they will have owned the bonds for only five months. The $15,000 credit to interest expense is a return, in advance, of one month's interest ($3,000,000 × 6% × 1/12).

(*Continued on page 66*)

EXPLANATIONS

Current liabilities are those which are due within the operating cycle of the business, or one year, whichever period is longer. Any liability not included as current is generally designated long-term. Certain items, such as contingent liabilities, where material, are disclosed as a footnote to the financial statements.

1. *Notes receivable discounted* is a contingent liability and is shown in a footnote.

2. *Accounts payable for goods in transit* is a current liability since in most instances title will pass at the point of shipment.

3. Since the outcome of a *pending lawsuit* is in doubt, no recognition can be given in the statements.

4. *Employees' taxes withheld* is a current liability of the employer (business entity).

5. *Temporary borrowings from affiliates,* since they can be expected to be repaid within the year, are reflected as a current liability.

6. *Maturing bonds which are to be refunded,* are classified as a long-term liability.

7. *Current sinking fund installment of long-term mortgage bonds,* since it will be due within the current year, will be shown as a current liability.

8. *Firm commitment for purchase of materials* is classified as a contingent liability and is shown as a footnote to the financial statement.

9. *Accrued liabilities* are amounts owed but not yet payable (e.g., accrued salaries); normally they would be current.

Answers

c	1
a	2
c	3
a	4
a	5
b	6
a	7
c	8
a	9

Date	Account	Debit	Credit
10. March 1, 1967	Cash	1,025,000.00	
	Bonds payable		1,000,000.00
	Accrued bond interest payable		10,000.00
	Premium on bonds payable		15,000.00
	To record issuance of $1,000,000 par value bonds at 101½ plus accrued interest.		
July 1, 1967	Accrued bond interest payable	10,000.00	
	Interest expense	20,000.00	
	Cash		30,000.00
	To record payment of semi-annual bond interest due on $1,000,000 par value bonds outstanding.		
July 1, 1967	Cash	816,000.00	
	Bonds payable		800,000.00
	Premium on bonds payable		16,000.00
	To record issuance of $800,000 par value bonds at 102.		
December 31, 1967	Interest expense	54,000.00	
	Accrued interest payable		54,000.00
	To accrue liability for semi-annual interest due January 1, 1968 on $1,800,000 of par value bonds outstanding.		
December 31, 1967	Premium on bonds payable	2,113.28	
	Interest expense		2,113.28

To amortize premium on bonds as follows:

$$10/118 \times 15{,}000 = 1{,}271.18$$
$$6/114 \times 16{,}000 = 842.10$$
$$\underline{\underline{2{,}113.28}}$$

Date	Account	Debit	Credit
December 31, 1967	Revenue and expense summary	71,886.72	
	Interest expense		*71,886.72*
	To close bond interest to expense revenue and expense summary.		
January 1, 1968	Accrued interest payable	54,000.00	
	Cash		54,000.00
	To record payment of semi-annual bond interest due on $18,000 par value bonds outstanding.		
January 1, 1968	Bond payable	300,000.00	
	Premium on bonds payable	4,814.45	
	Cash		303,000.00
	Gain on Bond Retirement		1,814.45
	To record purchase of 300,000 par value of company's own bonds at 101 plus accrued interest.		

Note: 1/6 of unamortized bond premium of $28,886.72 is written off (300,000/1,800,000).

situation, the buyer must pay to the issuing corporation (seller) the interest accrued to the date of sale.

Adjusting Entries. At the end of each accounting period, the bond discount or bond premium account must be amortized by an appropriate debit or credit to interest expense. The amount of accrued interest must also be journalized.

Balance Sheet Presentation of Bonded Indebtedness. The bond discount may be treated as a *deferred charge* item in the asset section or as a deduction from the bonds payable in the long-term liabilities section. Similarly, the bond premium may be treated as a *deferred credit* or as an addition to the bonds payable.

Operation of a Bond Sinking Fund. The bond indenture may contain a provision that a special fund, termed a sinking fund, be created for the accumulation of money necessary to redeem the bonds at maturity. Periodic payments of cash are made to the sinking fund, which usually is administered by an independent trustee. This cash is invested in income-paying securities. The cash, plus the earned income, should equal the principal amount of bonds to be retired.

Bond Indenture Restrictions on Dividends. As an additional measure of protection for the bondholders, the bond indenture may call for limitations on the payment of dividends by the corporation. If such a limitation is established, a note detailing the facts should be made part of the financial statements.

Types of Bonds. Bonds will differ as to their provisions. Some of these features are noted below:

1. *Mortgage Bonds*—Secured, real and/or personal properties are pledged as security.

2. *Debenture Bonds*—Offer to holders no specific security. Only the general credit of the corporation backs a debenture bond issue.

3. *Registered and Coupon Bonds*—A record of the name and address of the owner of registered bonds is maintained by the issuer and interest payments are made directly to the owner of record. Coupon bonds (bearer bonds) have interest coupons attached to the bond certificate.

4. *Convertible Bonds*—May be exchanged for other securities of the issuing corporation under specified conditions.

5. *Callable Bonds*—The issuing corporation has the right to make payment prior to maturity at a specific price.

Adjusting Entries. The facts in the preceding illustrative case require the following entries on June 30th:

1. Premium on bonds payable	3,782	
Interest expense		3,782

To amortize bond premium for the period ended June 30 (5/119 90,000 = 3,781.51).

2. Interest expense	90,000	
Accrued interest payable		90,000

To record bond interest for the six month period ended June 30, payable July 1st.

Operation of a Bond Sinking Fund. A few of the typical transactions involving sinking funds are the following:

1. Sinking fund cash	100,000	
Cash		100,000

To record the annual cash deposited with the trustee.

2. Sinking fund securities	96,000	
Sinking fund cash		96,000

To record the purchase of securities by the trustee.

3. Sinking fund cash	3,750	
Sinking fund income		3,750

To record the interest and dividends received on sinking fund investments.

4. Sinking fund cash	908,500	
Sinking fund securities		896,000
Gain on sale of investments		12,500

To record the sale of sinking fund securities by the trustee.

5. The cash now available in the fund (assume $1,004,000) would be utilized to pay the bonds at maturity:

Bonds payable	1,000,000	
Cash	4,000	
Sinking fund cash		1,004,000

6. *Sinking Fund Bonds*—A fund must be created to accumulate the necessary money to retire the bonds at maturity. The sinking fund may be under the control of the issuing corporation or of a special trustee.

7. *Term and Serial Bonds*—When all the bonds of an issue mature at the same time, the bonds are referred to as term bonds. If there are several maturity dates, the bonds are termed serial bonds.

Contingent Liabilities. Various situations, such as discounting notes receivable, create a potential liability to the corporation. Future events will either result in the elimination of all liability or the creation of a real liability. This possible future obligation is known as a *contingent liability.* In most instances, contingent obligations are disclosed in footnotes to the financial statements.

17 VOUCHER SYSTEM

SELF-TEST

DIRECTIONS: Write your answers (T or F) on the numbered lines to the right. To check your answers, turn to page 69.

1. The voucher register replaces the cash disbursements journal.
2. The voucher is prepared by the vendor when the merchandise is shipped.
3. The accounts payable subsidiary ledger is eliminated in a voucher system of accounting.
4. C. O. D. items require entry in the voucher register.
5. The voucher system provides a history of the business done with a particular supplier.
6. The check register is used in the voucher system as a substitute for the cash disbursements journal.
7. The original voucher must be cancelled when a credit is taken against a supplier's invoice.
8. Partial payments can be made when a voucher system is being used.
9. A "voucher" is the same thing as an "invoice."
10. Internal control is usually improved when a voucher system is used.

1 ______
2 ______
3 ______
4 ______
5 ______
6 ______
7 ______
8 ______
9 ______
10 ______

BASIC FACTS

Elements of the Voucher System. The voucher system is an accounting method of exercising control over the disbursement of cash from a business. When the *voucher register* is used, it replaces the purchase journal and the accounts payable subsidiary ledger. The system has as its nucleus an accounting document called a *voucher*. This term refers to a document that is prepared by the purchaser and on which is recorded all of the pertinent data relating to the liability. Each invoice received by an enterprise, whether for merchandise purchased, services rendered, or any other expense item, serves as the basis for the voucher.

It is a necessary part of the voucher system that: (1) all supporting documentation, such as purchase orders and receiving reports, be compared with the invoiced amounts to establish the accuracy of prices and quantities shown; and (2) the accounting department verify the arithmetical accuracy of the dollar amount of the invoice.

When these two steps have been performed, the details of the transaction are entered on the voucher which is transmitted, with the invoice and all supporting documentation, to the financial officer having authority to approve payment. Once the voucher is approved, it is recorded in the voucher register. This register serves a function similar to the purchase journal and is a source of posting to the general ledger. Under a voucher system, a voucher *must* be prepared for *all* invoices, even those for which immediate payment is to be made. A check cannot be disbursed unless a voucher authorizing payment has been prepared. Vouchers must be numbered in consecutive order and the number of each voucher appears in the voucher register. The voucher number is significant because under the system, liabilities are not accumulated by the vendor. Each unpaid voucher stands alone and the voucher number is a means of identifying the

(*Continued on page 70*)

ILLUSTRATIONS AND EXAMPLES

Typical Voucher

VOUCHER

MARC RICHARDS AND COMPANY

Date ______________________ Voucher No. ______________________

Payee ______________________ Date Due ______________________

____

Invoice No. ______________________ Invoiced Amount $ ______________________

Invoice Date ______________________ Terms ______________________

APPROVAL

Quantities checked to receiving ticket ______________________

Prices checked to purchase order ______________________

Extensions verified ______________________

Approved for payment ______________________

Voucher—Face

EXPLANATIONS

1. *The voucher register* does not *replace the cash disbursements journal;* it replaces the purchase journal and the accounts payable subsidiary ledger. The cash disbursements journal is still used in a modified form called a check register.

2. *The voucher is* not *prepared by the vendor when the merchandise is shipped.* The purchaser prepares the voucher, taking the information from the supplier's invoice.

3. *The accounts payable subsidiary ledger is eliminated in a voucher system of accounting.*

4. *C. O. D. items require entry in the voucher register.* The basic concept of the voucher system requires that all invoices be entered in the voucher register.

5. *The voucher system* does not *provide a history of the business done with a particular supplier.* This information is provided only when a purchases journal and an accounts payable subsidiary ledger card is used.

6. *The check register is used in the voucher system as a substitute for the cash disbursements journal.*

7. *The original voucher must be cancelled when a credit is taken against a supplier's invoice.*

8. *Partial payments can be made when a voucher system is being used.* Partial payments are cumbersome to handle but they can fit into a voucher system. The procedure is to cancel the original voucher and prepare two or more new vouchers, each in the amount of the individual payments to be made.

9. *A "voucher"* is not *the same as an "invoice."* A voucher is a form used with the voucher system to which invoices, shipping documents, and receipts are attached. Terms of settlement, authority for payment, and distribution of expense are also included on the voucher.

10. *Internal control is usually improved when a voucher system is used.*

Answers

F	1
F	2
T	3
T	4
F	5
T	6
T	7
T	8
F	9
T	10

Account Distribution

Amount

Purchases ______ $
Freight in ______
Supplies ______
Repairs ______
Advertising ______
Delivery expense ______

Credit vouchers payable $______

Distribution approved ______

Voucher No. ______

Payee ______

Date ______
Purchase date ______

Invoice amount ______ $
Discount ______
Adjustment ______
Net amount ______ $______

Paid on ______
Check No. ______
Recorded ______

Voucher-back

unpaid vouchers. Vouchers are filed in an unpaid voucher file until payment is made. At the time of payment, the vouchers are removed from the file and cancelled or mutilated so that they cannot be re-used. Special columns are provided in the voucher register to record payment of a voucher. At any given point of time the unpaid vouchers can be determined by taking a total of the "open" or unpaid amounts. This total should always agree with the total of the vouchers in the unpaid voucher file.

Since every item requiring an outlay of cash is recorded in the books through the voucher system, a multi-column cash disbursements journal is unwarranted. Instead, a simplified version of the disbursements journal, known as the *check register*, is used. This book of original entry will usually have three money columns, a debit column to vouchers payable, and credit columns to purchase discounts and cash.

Items Requiring Special Treatment. The voucher system performs best when each invoice is paid in full, without any adjustment for returns or other allowances. This is due to the fact that there is no subsidiary ledger account to accumulate partial payments, or to record returns. Since partial payments, returns and allowances are expected occurrences in business, the voucher register must be able to accommodate these types of transactions.

Partial Payments. When it is the intention to pay an invoice in two or more installments, a separate voucher should be prepared for each installment. If it is decided to make partial payments after the voucher has been prepared and recorded, proper treatment would require the cancellation of the old voucher and the preparation of two or more new vouchers. The first voucher should be for the amount of the installment to be paid, the remaining balance is recorded on a separate voucher(s) (see the first, fourth, and fifth lines of the illustrated voucher register).

Purchase Returns. If a credit is to be taken against a supplier's invoice, the original voucher must be cancelled and a new voucher prepared for the corrected amount (see the second and seventh lines of the illustrated voucher register).

Advantages and Disadvantages of Voucher System. The voucher system has received wide acceptance, especially by large enterprises concerned with adequate internal control procedures. When compared to a purchase journal with an accounts payable subsidiary ledger, it has some disadvantages of a minor nature.

Advantages

1. The immediate recording of invoices provides for the charge to be recorded on the books in the period incurred.

2. The voucher provides a history of an expenditure.

3. The absence of subsidiary ledgers saves enormous bookkeeping details.

4. The verification and approval built into the system insure that only valid obligations are recorded and paid.

Disadvantages

1. The lack of a subsidiary ledger does not permit the determination of the amount of business done with a supplier.

2. Procedures to handle partial payments and returns are somewhat burdensome.

VOUCHER REGISTER

Date	Voucher No.	Payee	Payment		Vouchers Payable (Credit)	Purchases (Debit)	Supplies (Debit)	Advertising (Debit)	Sundry Accounts		
			Date	Check No.					Account	Ref.	Amount
1966											
Sept. 1	515	Continental Company	See Voucher Nos. 518, 519		750.00	750.00					
1	516	Smith and Jones	See Voucher No. 521		300.00	300.00					
3	517	Acme Realty Co.	9-3-66	1430	1,000.00				Rent	453	1,000.00
4	518	Continental Company	9-8-66	1444	350.00				Vouchers Payable	215	750.00
4	519	Continental Company			400.00						
5	520	Metropolitan Water Co.	9-20-66	1480	100.00				Water	463	100.00
9	521	Smith and Jones	9-15-66	1463	250.00				Vouchers Payable	215	300.00
									Purchase Returns and Allowances	410	(50.00)
…	…	…	…	…	…	…	…	…	…	…	…
30	553	RFM Merchandise Sales			1,350.00	1,350.00					
30	554	Tri-Master Company	9-30-66	1501	87.00		87.00				
					23,500.00	18,750.00	490.00	1,450.00			2,810.00
					(215)	(401)	(415)	(925)			(√)

18 DEPARTMENTAL OPERATIONS HOME OFFICE AND BRANCH ACCOUNTING

SELF-TEST

Prime Manufacturing Company manufactures kitchen appliances in St. Louis, Missouri. The home office is located in St. Louis and sales offices are maintained in various cities throughout the country. Prime maintains a decentralized accounting system.

1. Prepare the necessary journal entries to record the following transactions on the books of the home office and the branch.

2. Prepare adjusting and closing entries.

3. Prepare financial statements for the branch.

July 1. The home office transfers $5,000 in cash to provide the branch with working capital.
July 2. The branch purchases $2,000 worth of office equipment for cash.
July 6. Merchandise costing $12,000 is shipped to the branch from the home office.
July 12. The branch purchases space in the Sunday edition of the local newspaper for $1,200; office stationery and supplies are purchased for $185.
July 14. Cash of $6,500 is transferred to the branch from the home office.
July 15. Sales on account are made in the amount of $2,500 by the branch.
July 15. Branch incures operating expenses of $2,375.
July 16. Branch pays semi-monthly payroll of $1,850.
July 18. Sales on account are made in the amount of $5,600.
July 21. Advertising expense of $1,200 is paid by branch (see July 12th).
July 22. Cash of $1,500 is collected on accounts receivable.
July 28. Branch sales on account are made in the amount of $7,800; cash sales are made in the amount of $640.
July 31. Branch pays semi-monthly payroll of $1,850. Inventory of branch at July 31 is $4,100.

To check your answers, turn to page 73.

BASIC FACTS

Departmental Operations. In many organizations with diverse operations, activities are organized along departmental lines. The accounting records must provide information in order for management to measure departmental efficiency.

There are various methods of allocating expenses. The gross profit may be determined for each department by segregating merchandise inventory, purchases, purchases returns and allowances, and sales and sales returns and allowances. The journals would provide separate departmental columns. Further refinement may be made by determining net income for each department. This requires that certain expenses, e.g., rent, heat, light and power, and executive salaries be allocated. Bases of allocation include floor space, sales dollars, number of employees, and cost of equipment.

Another method suggested by many accountants is the use of the departmental margin or contribution margin. Under this method all direct expenses (those clearly assignable) are charged to the department and indirect expenses are not allocated.

Operation of Branches. A branch can be defined as a unit of an existing business, operating at a location separate from the main (home) unit. Branch operations are often associated with the retail trade and service business. Financial organizations also utilize branches.

Centralized vs. Decentralized Accounting. There are two methods or systems used in accounting for branch operations. The *centralized accounting method* limits the branches' responsibility to the preparation of supporting documents, such as sales invoices and vouchers, which are transmitted to the home office. The branch does not maintain a separate set of books; its activities are incorporated in the journals and ledgers of the home office. This system has the advantage of minimizing bookkeeping costs. However, there are delays in recording branch activities that do not exist when a *decentralized accounting system* is used. Under the latter system, the branch maintains a separate set of books. Since the branch is not a separate entity, there can be no regular capital accounts; instead, a *home office account* takes the place of the stockholders' equity accounts.

Reciprocal Account Concept. The home office and branch books combine to make a complete set of books for the entity. On the home office ledger an account is maintained for each branch. The balance in the account represents the excess (or deficiency) of assets over liabilities for the branch involved. On the branch's ledger a reciprocal account for the home office is maintained. These accounts are reciprocal in that they are equal but have opposite balances (i.e., one a debit, one a credit) (Fig. 1).

The home office records a transfer of assets to the branch by crediting the applicable asset accounts and debiting the branch account. A *shipment to branch account* is credited in lieu of a reduction to merchandise inventory. The assets are debited on the branch books. Shipments from home office is debited to record the inventory transferred. The reciprocal accounts are in balance (Fig. 2, entry 1).

A cash transfer affects the home office investment in the branch and therefore must be recorded on both sets of books (Fig. 2, entry 5).

At the end of the accounting period, the branch will close the income and expense accounts to an *expense and revenue summary*, which is then closed to the *home office account* (Fig. 2, entry 6).

The branch net income will be closed to profit and loss on the home office books.

Home Office and Branch Office Combined Financial Statements. Separate financial statements—balance sheet and income statement—may be prepared for the home office and each branch. The individual branch statements are used by management to determine operating efficiency on a unit basis.

The transactions of the particular branch are of little interest to creditors and stockholders and therefore branch statements are rarely published. A combined income statement and balance sheet is prepared for the home office and branches. Work sheets are prepared to combine accounts; reciprocal accounts are eliminated from the combined statements.

Fig. 1 Reciprocal Account Concept

Home Office Books		*Albany Branch's Books*		*Buffalo Branch's Books*	
Branch–Albany		Assets		Assets	
(A) 50,000		150,000		60,000	
Branch–Buffalo		Liabilities		Liabilities	
	15,000 (B)		100,000		75,000
		Home Office Account		Home Office Account	
			50,000 (A)	(B) 15,000	

ANSWERS

1.

Date	Home Office Books	Dr.	Cr.	Branch A Books	Dr.	Cr.
July 1	Branch A	5,000		Cash	5,000	
	Cash		5,000	Home office		5,000
July 2				Office equipment	2,000	
				Cash		2,000
July 6	Branch A	12,000		Shipments from home office	12,000	
	Shipments to branch		12,000	Home office		12,000
July 12				Advertising	1,200	
				Office supplies	185	
				Accounts payable		1,385
July 14	Branch A	6,500		Cash	6,500	
	Cash		6,500	Home office		6,500
July 15				Accounts receivable	2,500	
				Sales		2,500
July 15				Operating expenses	2,375	
				Accounts payable		2,375
July 16				Payroll	1,850	
				Cash		1,850
July 18				Accounts receivable	5,600	
				Sales		5,600
July 21				Accounts payable	1,200	
				Cash		1,200
July 22				Cash	1,500	
				Accounts receivable		1,500
July 28				Accounts receivable	7,800	
				Cash	640	
				Sales		8,440
July 31				Payroll	1,850	
				Cash		1,850

(Continued on Page 74)

Fig. 2 Typical Transactions

Transaction	Home Office Books			Branch Books–Albany		
(1) Transfer by home office of $2,500 in cash, furniture & fixtures with a cost of $7,000, and inventory of $15,000.	Branch–Albany	24,500		Cash	2,500	
	Cash		2,500	Shipment from home office	15,000	
	Furniture & fixtures		7,000	Furniture & fixtures	7,000	
	Shipment to branch–Albany		15,000	Home office account		$24,500
(2) The branch purchased merchandise on account for $10,000 and paid general expense of $1,000				Purchases	10,000	
				General expenses	1,000	
				A/c payable		10,000
				Cash		1,000
(3) Merchandise was sold on account for $15,000.				A/c receivable	15,000	
				Sales		15,000
(4) $10,000 in cash was received from customer				Cash	10,000	
				A/c receivable		10,000
(5) The branch remitted $5,000 to the home office	Cash	5,000		Home office account	5,000	
	Branch–Albany		5,000	Cash		5,000
(6) To record branch–Albany's income of $5,000	Branch Albany	5,000		Expense & revenue summary	5,000	
	Branch Albany net income		5,000	Home office		5,000

2.

Adjusting and Closing Entries

July 31	Merchandise inventory		4,100	
	Sales		16,540	
	Expense and revenue summary			20,640
July 31	Expense and revenue summary		19,460	
	Payroll			3,700
	Operating expense			2,375
	Advertising			1,200
	Office supplies			185
	Shipments from home office			12,000

July 31	Branch A	1,180	
	Branch A net income		1,180

Expense and revenue summary	1,180	
Home office		1,180

3.

Branch A

Statement of Assets, Liabilities and Home Office

July 31, 19__

Assets		*Liabilities and Home Office*	
Cash	6,740	Liabilities-accounts payable	2,560
Accounts receivable	14,400		
Merchandise inventory	4,100	Home office	24,680
Office equipment	2,000		
Total assets	27,240	Total liabilities and home office	27,240

Branch A

Statement of Income

For the Month of July, 19__

Sales		16,540
Cost of sales		
Shipments from home office	12,000	
less inventory, July 31, 19__	4,100	7,900
Gross profit on sales		8,640
Expenses:		
Payroll	3,700	
Operating expenses	2,375	
Advertising	1,200	
Office supplies	185	7,460
Net income		1,180

19 MANUFACTURING OPERATIONS

SELF-TEST

DIRECTIONS: For questions 1-11, write your answers (T or F) on the numbered lines to the right. To check your answers, turn to page 77.

1. Indirect manufacturing costs are includible in inventory valuation.
2. Variable administrative expenses are properly included in product costs under absorption costing.
3. Inventories priced under direct costing methods will result in lower inventory valuations than those under absorption costing methods.
4. Manufacturing burden can be eliminated through increased production efficiency.
5. Material, labor, and overhead are the main elements of manufacturing cost.

In questions 6-11, is the item included in the "cost of goods manufactured" statement?

6. Raw materials.
7. Indirect labor.
8. Finished goods inventory.
9. Depreciation of office equipment.
10. Machinery repairs.
11. Advertising expense.

1 ________
2 ________
3 ________
4 ________
5 ________
6 ________
7 ________
8 ________
9 ________
10 ________
11 ________

The following is a partial trial balance of XYZ Corporation for the year ended December 31, 19__.

12. Prepare a Statement of Cost of Goods Manufactured.
13. Prepare a partial Income Statement through Gross Profit.

	Debits	Credits
Advertising	18,000	
Administrative salaries	48,000	
Amortization of patents	6,000	
Bad debts	3,400	
Depreciation–building (80% applicable to factory building)	1,600	
Depreciation–furniture and fixtures	1,200	
Depreciation–machinery and equipment	2,400	
Direct labor	249,000	
Heat, light and power (20% applicable to non-manufacturing use)	15,000	
Indirect labor	42,000	
Interest expense	950	
Miscellaneous factory costs	12,000	
Miscellaneous selling expense	15,000	
Property taxes (80% applicable to factory)	10,500	
Purchase returns and allowances		4,500
Raw material purchases	194,000	
Research and development costs	6,500	
Sales		791,000
Sales returns and allowances	7,450	
Transportation in	3,500	
Telephone and telegraph	7,400	
Raw materials inventory–beginning of period	23,000	
Raw materials inventory–end of period		18,500
Work in process inventory–beginning of period	24,500	
Work in process inventory–end of period		28,000
Finished goods inventory–beginning of period	78,500	
Finished goods inventory–end of period		69,500

To check your answers, turn to page 79.

BASIC FACTS

Manufacturing Costs. A manufacturing operation has special accounting problems unlike those of merchandising or service organizations. Labor and machinery are used in the manufacturing process to convert materials into finished goods; in addition, a wide variety of overhead expenses will be incurred. Production is a vital element of a manufacturing business and the accounting records must provide for the determination of the various production costs.

Manufacturing costs are includible in determination of inventory valuation; selling, general, and administrative expenses are charged to profit and loss. Manufacturing costs are divided into three categories:

1. *Raw Materials* (Direct Materials) are those materials that enter into and become part of the manufactured article. The statement of cost of goods manufactured details a computation of the raw materials used.

2. *Direct Labor* consists of that portion of the factory cost which can be directly identified with a specific manufacturing job or process. *Indirect Labor*, which cannot be identified with a special manufacturing job or process, is considered as factory overhead. It includes wages of foremen, storekeepers, inspectors, and timekeepers, as well as sick pay and idle time of direct factory workers.

3. *Factory Overhead*, known variously as manufacturing expense, burden, or overhead, includes all the costs of manufacturing other than direct material and direct labor. Included are: all items of equipment maintenance; indirect materials (shop supplies, lubricants); depreciation; heat, light, and power; and special service department costs (purchasing department, storekeeping department). If an expense item applies to the factory operation as well as to administrative or sales department, a fair method of allocation must be established.

Types of Costs. Cost may be classified in various ways for purposes of analysis and report presentation. Several of the classifications are discussed below.

Product Costs and Period Costs. It is an accepted accounting principle that revenues of a period should be charged with those costs which are reasonably *associated with the product* represented by such revenue. Unfortunately, there is no general acceptance as to which costs are "associated with the product" and which should be immediately charged to revenues without passing through the inventory accounts. Exponents of *direct costing* would include only direct material, direct labor, and variable overhead costs in the definition of product costs. Exponents of *absorption costing* would include all costs of production as product costs. Use of direct costing is not an acceptable method for financial statement presentation.

Fixed, Variable, and Semi-Variable Costs. Costs may be categorized by their relationship to variability of production (output) or sales. Fixed costs tend to remain relatively constant with changes in output or sales (rent, depreciation, and insurance). Variable costs will be directly correlated to activity, such as direct materials and direct labor. Other costs, semi-variable in nature, will vary to some degree with activity changes (supervisory salaries and utility costs).

It must be pointed out that the classification of a cost as fixed, variable, or semi-variable may be dependent on policies and decisions of management. Depreciation based on an output calculation would mean that the depreciation expense is variable rather than fixed.

ILLUSTRATIONS AND EXAMPLES

Marc Richards, Inc.
Cost of Raw Materials Used
For the Year Ended December 31, 19__

Raw materials inventory, January 1, 19__			$25,000
Purchases		$150,000	
Less: Purchase discount	$2,000		
Purchase returns	1,000	3,000	147,000
Freight in			4,000
Cost of raw materials available			$176,000
Less: Raw materials inventory, December 31, 19__			22,000
Cost of raw materials used			$154,000

(*Continued on page 78*)

ANSWERS

12.

XYZ Corporation
Statement of Cost of Goods Manufactured
For the Year Ended December 31, 19__

Work in process inventory–beginning of period			$24,500
Raw materials			
Inventory–beginning of period		$23,000	
Purchases	$194,000		
Less: purchase returns and allowances	4,500	189,500	
Transportation in		3,500	
Cost of raw material available		216,000	
Less: raw material inventory–end of period		18,500	
Cost of raw material used		197,500	
Direct labor		249,000	
Manufacturing overhead			
Indirect labor	$42,000		
Heat, light, and power	12,000		
Property taxes	8,400		
Depreciation–building	1,280		
Depreciation–machinery and equipment	2,400		
Amortization of patents	6,000		
Research and development costs	6,500		
Miscellaneous factory costs	12,000	90,580	
			537,080
Total manufacturing costs			$561,580
Less: work in process inventory–end of period			28,000
Cost of goods manufactured			$533,580

Answers

T	1
F	2
T	3
F	4
T	5
T	6
T	7
F	8
F	9
T	10
F	11

13.

XYZ Corporation
Partial Income Statement
For the Year Ended December 31, 19__

Gross sales		$791,000
Less: sales returns and allowances		7,450
Net sales		783,550
Cost of goods sold		
Finished goods inventory–beginning of period	$ 78,500	
Cost of goods manufactured (separate statement)	533,580	
Cost of goods available for sale	612,080	
Less: finished goods inventory–end of period	69,500	
Cost of goods sold		542,580
Gross profit		$240,970

Marc Richards, Inc.

Statement of Cost of Goods Manufactured

For the Year Ended December 31, 19__

Work in process inventory, Jan. 1, 19__			$65,000
Cost of raw materials used (see Statement)		$154,000	
Direct Labor		180,000	
Factory overhead:			
Indirect labor	$35,000		
Heat, light, and power	15,000		
Depreciation–building	10,000		
Repairs and maintenance	7,000		
Sundry factory expense	5,000	72,000	
Total manufacturing costs			406,000
			$471,000
Less: Work in process inventory, Dec. 31, 19__			70,000
Cost of goods manufactured			$401,000

Marc Richards, Inc.

Income Statement

For the Year Ended December 31, 19__

Sales		$550,000
Cost of goods sold:		
Finished goods inventory, Jan. 1, 19__	$ 50,000	
Cost of goods manufactured (see Statement)	401,000	
Cost of goods available for sale	451,000	
Finished goods inventory, Dec. 31, 19__	66,000	
Cost of goods sold		385,000
Gross profit		$165,000
Selling, general, and administrative expenses		90,000
Net income		$ 75,000

20 COST ACCOUNTING

SELF-TEST

Post the following transactions directly to T accounts:

1. Beginning inventories:

Raw materials	$18,000
Work in process	25,000
Finished goods	32,000

2. Raw materials purchased on account $35,000.
3. Direct materials placed into production $33,000; indirect materials entering into production $3,000.
4. Labor costs incurred for the period total $15,000 (credit wages payable), of which $4,000 was for indirect labor.
5. Other factory overhead costs totaled $12,000 (credit cash).
6. Applied $20,000 of factory overhead to work in process.
7. Work in process completed amounted to $70,000.
8. Goods sold during the month, amounting to $85,000, cost $60,000.

To check your answers, turn to page 81.

BASIC FACTS

Definition and Purpose. Cost accounting is a system used to determine the cost of materials, labor, and overhead entering into the manufacture of a product for sale. Cost accounting enables management to make intelligent decisions in regard to the manufacturing process. By comparing actual costs with expected or standard costs, favorable or unfavorable variations can be determined and analyzed.

Cost Accounting Systems. There are two basic cost accounting systems. The decision as to which system to use will depend on the nature of the manufacturing process. The *job order cost system* is suitable for an operation which manufactures different products, either for special order or for stock. The *process cost system* is best used where there is continuous production of a single, homogeneous product. Under either system, an average unit cost is determined. The cost accounting system operates within the framework of the regular general ledger accounts. Transactions relating to the manufacturing process flow through special accounts that do not appear in the ledger of a mercantile or service business. Perpetual inventory records are usually maintained in manufacturing companies.

The Job Order Cost System. The special cost accounts are set up to match the cost flow with the flow of work. The first stage in the work flow is *purchasing*. The cost of materials, labor, and overhead items are charged to *raw materials*, *factory payroll control*, and *manufacturing overhead control* accounts respectively. As these costs are applied to the manufacturing process, they are removed from these accounts and are charged to the production accounts.

The second stage in the work flow is *production*. The various cost components (material, labor, and overhead) are debited to a production account, known as *work-in-process*, and credits are made to the appropriate account.

The third stage is *warehousing*. As goods are finished, the costs are transferred from the work-in-process account to the *finished goods* account.

(*Continued on page 82*)

ILLUSTRATIONS AND EXAMPLES

Job Order Cost System

The Cost Cycle.

Marc Richards Manufacturing Co., Inc.

Summary of Transactions Affecting Cost Accounts for the month of September, 19___.

(A) Direct materials are purchased during the month for $40,000. Indirect materials were purchased for $3,500.

(B) Labor costs for the month totaled $25,000; $21,000 for direct labor and $4,000 for indirect labor.

(C) Various overhead costs (factory rent, electricity, etc.) were incurred in the amount of $28,000.

(D) Direct materials placed into production totaled $35,000; indirect materials entering into production totaled $3,000.

(E) All labor costs are charged to production.

(F) Overhead is applied to production at 175% of direct labor.

(G) $79,500 of work-in-process is completed during the month.

(H, I) Goods sold during the month, totaling $65,000, cost $45,000.

		Debit	Credit
(A)	Raw materials	43,500	
	Accounts payable		43,500
(B)	Factory payroll control	25,000	
	Cash		25,000
(C)	Manufacturing overhead control	28,000	
	Accounts payable		28,000
(D)	Work in process	35,000	
	Manufacturing overhead control	3,000	
	Raw materials		38,000
(E)	Work in process	21,000	
	Manufacturing overhead control	4,000	
	Factory payroll control		25,000
(F)	Work in process	36,750	
	Manufacturing overhead control		36,750
(G)	Finished goods	79,500	
	Work in process		79,500
(H)	Accounts receivable	65,000	
	Sales		65,000
(I)	Cost of goods sold	45,000	
	Finished goods		45,000

Manufacturing Overhead Control

Debit	Credit
(C) 28,000	(F) 36,750
(D) 3,000	
(E) 4,000	

Sales

Debit	Credit
	(H) 65,000

Raw Materials

Debit	Credit
(A) 43,500	(D) 38,000

Cash

Debit	Credit
	(B) 25,000

(*Continued on page 81*)

ANSWERS

Raw Materials

(1) Balance	18,000	(3)	36,000
(2)	35,000		

Work in Process

(1) Balance	25,000	(7)	70,000
(3)	33,000		
(4)	11,000		
(6)	20,000		

Finished Goods

(1) Balance	32,000	(8)	60,000
(7)	70,000		

Accounts Payable

		(2)	35,000

Manufacturing Overhead Control

(3)	3,000	(6)	20,000
(4)	4,000		
(5)	12,000		

Wages Payable

		(4)	15,000

Cash

		(5)	12,000

Cost of Goods Sold

(8)	60,000		

Accounts Receivable

(8)	85,000		

Sales

		(8)	85,000

(Illustrations and Examples continued)

Work in Process

(D) 35,000	(G) 79,500
(E) 21,000	
(F) 36,750	

Accounts Receivable

(H) 65,000	

Finished Goods

(G) 79,500	(I) 45,000

Cost of Goods Sold

(I) 45,000	

Factory Payroll Control

(B) 25,000	(E) 25,000

Accounts Payable

	(A) 43,500
	(C) 28,000

(Continued on page 82)

The final stage is *sales*. The sale of goods requires an entry removing costs from the finished goods account to a *cost of goods sold* account.

Applying Overhead. If cost accounting is to function as an effective tool of management, it must provide current cost data. Usually, the total overhead costs are not conveniently available until the end of an accounting period (month or year). When a job is complete, the total cost should be available. It is essential, therefore, that there be a method of estimating the overhead costs applicable to a particular job quickly and reliably. A method has been devised which relates the total expected overhead costs to a known factor of the manufacturing process. One of the most commonly used relationships is overhead cost to direct labor cost. Other bases sometimes used are direct labor hours, machine hours, or material costs.

Under-Applied and Over-Applied Overhead. In the previous section it was indicated that the application of overhead is based on estimates. At the end of any accounting period there is very little likelihood that the *applied* overhead will exactly equal the amount of *actual* overhead. The difference is referred to as *over-applied* (amounts charged to the jobs are greater than actual costs) or *under-applied* (actual costs are greater than amounts charged) overhead. There are several methods for the disposition of this variance. Two of these methods are: (1) Allocate to the products manufactured during the year. Some of the goods are still in process, others are on hand as finished goods, while still others have been sold. The under- or over-applied overhead is allocated, therefore, to work-in-process, finished goods, and cost of goods sold. (2) The under- or over-applied overhead is charged to cost of goods sold.

Process Cost System. Under a job order cost system an exact cost is established for each particular job. In a manufacturing operation where goods are mass produced and all items are identical, it is not necessary to determine exact costs for a specific item. The process cost system provides for a method of computing an *average unit cost.*

The flow of costs in a process cost system is identical to that of a job order system. Material, labor, and overhead items flow through the work-in-process accounts to finished goods accounts and to the cost of goods sold accounts. A reasonable method for applying overhead to production must be arrived at so that production accounts will be charged for the anticipated overhead expense. At the end of an accounting period the costs accumulated for a department are compared with the units produced, to arrive at an average unit cost.

Equivalent Production. In a going business it is very likely that at the end of any accounting period there will be goods in various stages of completion. Since the basis underlying process costs is the use of averages, it is necessary to determine the number of equivalent units produced.

Standard Costs. The use of standard costs gives management the opportunity to maximize efficiency by comparing actual and projected costs. Standard costs are scientifically predetermined estimates.

Variances. Differences between actual and standard costs are termed variances. Variances may be favorable (actual cost is less than standard) or unfavorable (actual cost is greater than standard). Variances can exist in each of the three cost elements—direct materials, direct labor, and manufacturing overhead.

Applying Overhead

Assume that a company expects to incur manufacturing overhead of $250,000 during its next fiscal year. During the same period, direct labor is expected to be $500,000. The ratio of overhead to direct labor is 50%. For each dollar of direct labor expense charged to a job, fifty cents of overhead should be applied. Job #450 with $4,500 of direct labor will be charged with $2,250 of applied overhead (4500 x 50%).

Process Cost System

Computation of Equivalent Production

Beginning inventory—Department 2 1,000 units 40% completed
Completed and transferred to finished goods . . . . 8,000 units
Ending inventory—Department 2 . . 500 units 30% completed

Equivalent units of production for period:

To process beginning inventory 1,000 units x 60%	600 units
Units started and completed (8,000 units less 1,000 units from beginning inventory)	7,000 units
To process ending inventory 500 units x 30%	150 units
	7,750 units

21 FUNDS STATEMENTS and CONSOLIDATED STATEMENTS

SELF-TEST

The following information is submitted, relating to Marc Richards & Company. Exhibt A reflects changes in balance sheet accounts during the year. Exhibit B is the income statement for the calendar year.

1. Prepare a work sheet for statement of source and application of funds. (To check your answer, turn to page 85.)

2. Prepare a statement of source and application of funds. (To check your answer, turn to page **100**.)

Exhibit A

Debit balance accounts	*Debit*	*Credit*
Cash	$ 4,700	
Notes receivable	1,500	
Accounts receivable		$ 280
Merchandise inventory	3,800	
Prepaid expenses		900
Furniture and equipment	6,800	
Credit balance accounts		
Allowance for bad debts		150
Allowance for depreciation– Furniture and equipment		2,270
Notes payable		3,800
Accounts payable	1,200	
Federal income tax payable		1,500
Dividends payable		800
Accrued expenses		100
Capital stock		3,500
Retained earnings		4,700
	$18,000	$18,000

Exhibit B

MARC RICHARDS & COMPANY
Statement of Income
For the Year Ended December 31, 19–

Sales		$41,000
Cost of goods sold	$22,730	
Selling and administration expenses	8,500	
Depreciation of furniture and equipment	2,370	
Provision for bad debts	150	
Loss on sale of furniture	250	
Provision for federal income tax	1,500	
	$35,500	$41,000
Net income	5,500	
	$41,000	$41,000

Additional Information:

(a) Dividends were declared in the amount of $800.
(b) Equipment purchased at a cost of $7,400.
(c) Furniture with a cost of $600, on which depreciation of $100 was taken, was sold for $250.
(d) Capital stock was sold for $3,500.

3. Prepare the journal entry to record the elimination of the investment account on the parent company's books at date of acquisition. Investment account is carried at cost. (To check your answer, turn to page **100**.

Subsidiary Company's Equity Section (at date of acquisition)	*Case A*	*Case B*	*Case C*	*Case D*	*Case E*
Capital stock, $10 par	$60,000	$60,000	$60,000	$60,000	$60,000
Retained earnings (deficit)	$20,000	$20,000	($10,000)	($10,000)	$40,000
Percentage of subsidiary's stock acquired	100%	80%	90%	90%	80%
Cost of acquisition	$80,000	$64,000	$45,000	$40,000	$95,000

BASIC FACTS

Definition of "Funds". The term *funds*, in an accounting or financial context, most commonly means *working capital* – the excess of current assets over current liabilities. The *source and application of funds statement,* or *funds statement,* accounts for variations in working capital.

Objectives of the Funds Statement. The principal purpose of the funds statement is to provide information not readily obtainable from the basic accounting statements (balance sheet and income statement). Although the statement is similar to the income statement in that it reports the results of operations for a given period of time, it is not a mere recording of income and expense items. The funds statement presents a review of the financial activities that have resulted in changes in the current position. Through analysis of changes to the *non-current accounts,* the source and disposition of the resources of the business are determined.

Sources of Funds. Any transaction that increases the working capital of an enterprise would be a source of funds. Items of this type result from:

An Increase (debit) to a Current Asset; a *credit* to a non-working capital account. Examples include the sale of merchandise, sale of fixed assets, and issuance of the company's capital stock or bonds. The amount of funds provided is the sales price obtained, rather than the book value of the asset sold.

A Decrease (debit) to a Current Liability; a *credit* to a non-working capital account. Examples include forgiveness of loan by corporate shareholder and refinancing of maturing loan with new long-term debt.

Application of Funds. Any transaction that decreases the working capital of an enterprise would be a disposition of funds. Items of this type result from:

A Debit to a Non-working Capital Account; an *increase* (credit) to a current liability account. Examples include the declaration of a cash dividend and purchase (on account) of fixed assets.

A Debit to a Non-working Capital Account; a *decrease* (credit) to a current asset account. Examples include the redemption of bonds or the retirement of capital stock.

Purpose of Consolidated Statement. In many instances a corporation will acquire a majority of the voting shares of a second corporation. When this occurs, a *parent-subsidiary* relationship is said to exist. The parent (controlling) corporation will carry as an investment on its books the cost of the subsidiary (controlled) corporation's stock. Although the two entities are legally separate and distinct, the element of control results in the creation of a *single economic unit.* To reflect this concept, it is often considered desirable to prepare financial statements which consolidate the operations and the assets and liabilities of both companies. Although practical control may be established through the ownership of only a small percentage of the voting shares, accountants usually re-

(*Continued on page 86.*)

ILLUSTRATIONS AND EXAMPLES

Marc Richards Inc.
Comparative Working Capital Schedule
December 31, 19–9 and 19–8

	December 31		Working Capital	
	19–9	19–8	Increase	Decrease
Current Assets				
Cash	$ 50,000	$ 45,000	$ 5,000	
Accounts receivable	75,000	82,000		$ 7,000
Inventories	150,000	130,000	20,000	
Prepaid expenses	8,000	7,000	1,000	
	$283,000	$264,000		
Current Liabilities				
Notes payable	$ 35,000	$ 40,000	$ 5,000	
Accounts payable	80,000	71,000		$ 9,000
	$115,000	$111,000		
Working capital	$168,000	$153,000	$31,000	$16,000
			16,000	
Increase in working capital			$15,000	

(*Continued on page 86.*)

ANSWERS

1.

Marc Richards & Company
Work Sheet For Statement of
Source and Application of Funds
For the Year Ended December 31, 19--

	YEAR'S CHANGES		ADJUSTMENTS		WORKING CAPITAL		FUNDS	
	Debit	Credit	Debit	Credit	Increase	Decrease	Applied	Provided
Cash	$ 4,700				$ 4,700			
Notes receivable	1,500				1,500			
Accounts receivable		$ 280				$ 280		
Merchandise inventory	3,800				3,800			
Prepaid expenses		900				900		
Furniture and equipment	6,800		(C)$ 600	(B)$7,400				
Allowance for bad debts		150				150		
Allowance for depreciation–furniture and equipment		2,270	(F) 2,370	(C) 100				
Notes payable		3,800				3,800		
Accounts payable	1,200				1,200			
Federal income tax payable		1,500				1,500		
Dividends payable		800				800		
Accrued expenses		100				100		
Capital stock		3,500	(D) 3,500					
Retained earnings		4,700	(E) 5,500	(A) 800				
	$18,000	$18,000						
Sales		$41,000						$41,000
Cost of goods sold	$22,730						$22,730	
Selling and administrative expenses	8,500						8,500	
Depreciation of furniture and equipment	2,370			(F) 2,370				
Provision for bad debts	150						150	
Loss on sale of furniture	250			(C) 250				
Provision for federal income tax	1,500						1,500	
	35,500	41,000						
Net income	5,500			(E) 5,500				
	$41,000	$41,000						
Sale of capital stock				(D) 3,500				3,500
Purchase of equipment			(B) 7,400				7,400	
Sale of furniture				(C) 250				250
Declaration of dividend			(A) 800				800	
					11,200	7,530	41,080	44,750
			$20,170	$20,170				
Increase In Working Capital						3,670	3,670	
					$11,200	$11,200	$44,750	$44,750

(Answers to problems 2 and 3 on page **100***.)*

quire ownership of 50% of the voting shares before consolidated statements are prepared. When consolidated statements are prepared, all inter-company balance sheet and income statement items must be eliminated.

Consolidated Balance Sheet. The Parent company may control a subsidiary by: (a) 100% ownership acquired at a cost equal to the book value of the subsidiary; (b) 100% ownership acquired at a cost above or below the book value of the subsidiary; (c) less than 100% ownership acquired at a cost equal to the book value; and (d) less than 100% ownership acquired at a cost above or below the book value.

The parent company will usually carry the investment in the subsidiary at cost. The worksheet elimination of the investment on the parent's books is made against the equity accounts on the subsidiary's books.

In the absence of any further acquisitions or disposals of the subsidiary's stock, the elimination entry (with few exceptions) will not change.

Consolidated Income Statement. Inter-company transactions such as sales, purchases, interest income and expense, rent income and expense, and service charge income and expense are eliminated in the preparation of the consolidated income statement. Inter-company gross profits in the beginning and ending inventories also require elimination.

Marc Richards Inc.
Statement of Source and Application of Funds
For the Year Ended December 31, 19–9

Source of Funds		
Operations:		
Net income for the year	$42,000	
Add: non-cash expense—depreciation of building and machinery	12,000	
From operations		$ 54,000
Sale of machinery (sales price)		22,000
Net proceeds from bond issue		24,000
Total sources of funds		$100,000
Application of Funds		
Purchase of land	$25,000	
Retirement of preferred stock	40,000	
Declaration of cash dividends	20,000	
Total application of funds		85,000
Increase in working capital		$ 15,000

The Investment Account Elimination:

S Corporation
Stockholders' Equity, December 31, 19–

Capital stock (10,000 shares outstanding)	$100,000
Retained earnings	40,000
Total stockholders' equity	$140,000

Case 1. "P" acquires 100% of the stock for $140,000.
2. "P" acquires 100% of the stock for $150,000.
3. "P" acquires 80% of the stock for $112,000.
4. "P" acquires 80% of the stock for $108,000.

	Case 1	*Case 2*	*Case 3*	*Case 4*
DR Capital stock–subsidiary	100,000	100,000	80,000	80,000
DR Retained earnings–subsidiary	40,000	40,000	32,000	32,000
DR Excess of cost of subsidiary over net assets acquired		10,000		
CR Excess of net assets acquired over cost of subsidiary stock				(4,000)
CR Investment in subsidiary	(140,000)	(150,000)	(112,000)	(108,000)

22 FINANCIAL STATEMENT ANALYSIS

SELF-TEST

DIRECTIONS: For questions 1-6, write your answer (a–n) on the numbered lines to the right. To check your answers to all questions, turn to page 89.

a sales	e equity	h inventory	k working capital
b acid test	f static	i vertical	l structural ratios
c preferred	g current	j trend ratios	m horizontal
d common-size statements			n common

1. ______________ analysis consists of a study of the behavior of each of the items in a financial statement with the passage of time.

2. Vertical analysis is considered to be a ____________ type of analysis because it is a study of relationships existing at a particualr date.

3. Common-size income statements present the various items as a percentage of ______________.

4. The acid test ratio assumes that ______________ will not be converted to cash in time to pay current liabilities.

5. Vertical, or static, measuring devices are ________ ________ and ______________.

6. The ______________ ratio indicates the portion of the assets supplied by the owners.

1 ________
2 ________
3 ________
4 ________
5 ________
6 ________

Marc Richards & Company
Comparative Balance Sheets December 31

Assets	*1968*	*1967*	*1966*
Cash	$ 24,000	$ 18,000	$ 14,000
Accounts receivable (net of allowance for bad debts)	120,000	130,000	128,000
Inventories	46,000	32,000	38,000
Total current assets	$190,000	$180,000	$180,000
Fixed assets (net of depreciation)	$102,000	$ 85,000	$ 60,000
Other non-current assets	8,000	5,000	10,000
Total non-current assets	$110,000	$ 90,000	$ 70,000
Total assets	$300,000	$270,000	$250,000
Liabilities and Capital			
Accounts payable	$ 80,000	$ 90,000	$ 70,000
Accrued expenses	18,000	15,000	9,000
Taxes payable	32,000	20,000	31,000
Total current liabilities	$130,000	$125,000	$110,000
Capital stock	$110,000	$100,000	$100,000
Retained earnings	60,000	45,000	40,000
Total capital	$170,000	$145,000	$140,000
Total liabilities and capital	$300,000	$270,000	$250,000

COMPUTE to the nearest one per cent the following *structural ratios* as of December 31, 1968:

7. Current ratio.
8. Acid test ratio.
9. Capital to liabilities.
10. Capital to non-current assets.

COMPUTE the following *trend ratios*, using 1966 as the base year (100%):

11. Current assets.
12. Current (total) liabilities.
13. Receivables.
14. Non-current assets.
15. Capital.

16. Prepare common-size balance sheets for the three years to the nearest tenth of one per cent.

BASIC FACTS

Purpose of Analysis. The term *financial statements* normally refers to the two basic accounting reports prepared at the end of an accounting period—the *balance sheet* and the *income statement*. The accountant must analyze the financial statements in order to interpret their meaning for management. Banks, trade creditors, employees, governmental agencies, and investors also require information that can be obtained only by applying analysis techniques to the financial statements.

Techniques and Procedures. The individual items that make up a financial statement have little significance standing alone. It is only when items are compared that meaningful conclusions can be drawn. The relationships developed between various elements of a statement are usually expressed as a percentage or as a ratio and are used as tools in the analysis process. Economic conditions and product acceptance are just two of the judgment factors that must also enter into any evaluation of a business entity.

Horizontal and Vertical Analysis. There are two general categories of measurements that are used in statement analysis. The first, *horizontal analysis*, measures the changes in corresponding items in successive statements. The second, *vertical analysis*, measures the relationships among the items in a single set of statements. Vertical analysis is a static analysis while horizontal analysis is dynamic since it measures changes through various periods of time. Neither type of analysis can be used to the exclusion of the other.

Common Size Statements. A common size statement is one which is prepared without dollar amounts. Instead, percentages are used and the result is a device for financial analysis. The common size balance sheet computes the ratio of each asset item to the total of assets and the ratio of each liability and capital item to the total of liabilities and capital. The common size income statement presents the various items as a percentage of the total revenues (gross sales).

Commonly Used Ratios.

Current Ratio. A determination of the relationship between current assets and

(*Continued on page 90*)

ILLUSTRATIONS AND EXAMPLES

Common Size Statements

Marc Richards, Inc.
Common Size Balance Sheet
September 30, 19__

ASSETS		*LIABILITIES AND CAPITAL*			
Current assets		*Current liabilities*			
Cash	5.1%	Notes payable			1.3%
Accounts receivable	22.3	Accounts payable			19.5
Merchandise inventory	38.4	Accrued expenses			9.7
Prepaid expenses	1.1				
Total current assets	66.9	Total current liabilities			30.5
Property		Long-term debt			13.6
Land	8.5	Total liabilities			44.1
Building, net of depreciation	24.6	Capital stock	48.3		
		Retained earnings	7.6		55.9
Total property	33.1				
Total assets	100.0%	Total liabilities and capital			100.0%

Marc Richards, Inc.
Common Size Income Statement
For Year Ended September 30, 19__

Sales	100.0%
Cost of sales	63.8
Gross profit on sales	36.2
Operating expenses	
General and administrative expenses	18.4
Sales expenses	10.3
	28.7
Operating income	7.5
Provision for federal income tax	4.6
Net income	2.9%

Current Ratio—Working Capital

	Year 1	*Year 2*
Current assets	$150,000	$300,000
Current liabilities	50,000	150,000
Working capital	$100,000	$150,000
Current ratio	300% or 3 to 1	200% or 2 to 1

Although the working capital increased by $50,000 in Year 2, from a determination of the current ratio it can be seen that the debt-paying ability (liquidity) of the entity has decreased, not improved.

(*Continued on page 90*)

ANSWERS

7. Current ratio–146%
8. Acid test ratio–111%
9. Capital to liabilities–131%
10. Capital to non-current assets–155%

	1968	*1967*	*1966*
11. Current assets	106%	100%	100%
12. Current (total) liabilities	118%	114%	100%
13. Receivables	94%	102%	100%
14. Non-current assets	157%	129%	100%
15. Capital	121%	104%	100%

16.

	1968	*1967*	*1966*
Assets			
Cash	8.0%	6.7%	5.6%
Accounts receivable (net of allowance for bad debts)	40.0%	48.1%	51.2%
Inventories	15.3%	11.9%	15.2%
Total current assets	63.3%	66.7%	72.0%
Fixed assets (net of depreciation)	34.0%	31.5%	24.0%
Other non-current assets	2.7%	1.8%	4.0%
Total assets	100.0%	100.0%	100.0%
Liabilities and Capital			
Accounts payable	26.7%	33.3%	28.0%
Accrued expenses	6.0%	5.6%	3.6%
Taxes payable	10.6%	7.4%	12.4%
Total current liabilities	43.3%	46.3%	44.0%
Capital stock	36.7%	37.0%	40.0%
Retained earnings	20.0%	16.7%	16.0%
Total capital	56.7%	53.7%	56.0%
Total liabilities and capital	100.0%	100.0%	100.0%

Answers

m 1

f 2

a 3

h 4

d, l 5

e 6

current liabilities. Used since the earliest days of financial statement analysis, it is an indication of an entity's debt-paying ability.

Working Capital. The amount of current assets not supplied by current creditors. It is computed by subtracting from current assets the amount of current liabilities.

Acid Test (Quick). An additional ratio to determine liquidity, computed by dividing the "quick assets" (all current assets, exclusive of merchandise inventory) by the amount of current liabilities. This ratio assumes that inventory will not be converted to cash in time to pay current liabilities.

Inventory Turnover. Inventory control is one of the most difficult tasks facing management. It is necessary that sufficient inventory be on hand to meet the demands of business. Overstocking of goods, with the resultant unproductive use of funds and the risk of inventory deterioration, must always be avoided.

Inventory turnover is computed by dividing the cost of goods sold by the average inventory. The turnover ratio (stated either in terms of days or the number of times per annum) is a measure of the merchandising efficiency of the entity.

Accounts Receivable.

Turnover. A measure of the efficiency in the collection of receivables, it is computed by dividing the "on account" sales by the average accounts receivable.

Number of Days' Sales in Receivables. Similar in purpose to the accounts receivable turnover, this measure is computed by dividing accounts receivable at year end by the average daily sales on account.

Since the days' sales in receivables gives an approximate indication of the length of time accounts receivable remain unpaid, it can be compared with credit terms and industry figures to establish efficiency in collecting receivables.

Net Sales to Total Assets. Net sales are divided by the average of the total assets at a measure of the effectiveness of asset utilization.

Equity to Debt. *Capitalization* of a corporation is a term used by investment analysts to indicate the total capital of a corporation plus the par value of any outstanding bonds. The term includes, therefore, items of paid-in capital and retained earnings. Analysts are interested in the relationship of the component parts of the capitalization of a corporation.

It is usually considered unsatisfactory if bondholders contribute too great a proportion of the total capitalization. Industrial organizations with bonds accounting for more than 25% of the capitalization usually are not considered satisfactorily capitalized by investment analysts. The *equity ratio*, which is computed by dividing the stockholders' equity by the total assets, indicates the portion of the assets supplied by the owners. There are no hard and fast ratios that can be applied to all businesses. Reasonable and judicious use of borrowed funds is desirable; management must decide to what extent it is advisable to substitute debt for equity.

Earnings Per Share. The amount earned per share of common stock is the amount of net income *available* for the common stockholders divided by the number of shares outstanding. The net income available to common stockholders is not synomous with net income where the corporation has preferred shares outstanding. Net income must first be reduced by the dividend requirements of the preferred shareholders.

Accounts Receivable—Number of Days' Sales in Receivables

Accounts receivable—end of year	$ 135,000
Net sales on account	$2,737,500
Average daily sales (net sales on account ÷ 365)	$ 7,500
Number of days' sales in receivables (accounts receivable—end of year ÷ average daily sales)	18

Equity to Debt

Bonds	$ 500,000	20%
Preferred stock	250,000	10%
Common stock and retained earnings	1,750,000	70%
	$2,500,000	100%

Earnings Per Share

Bonds (6%)	$ 300,000
Preferred stock (7%)	$ 500,000
Common stock (par $10)	$2,000,000
net income after bond interest of $18,000 and income taxes	$455,000
Preferred dividends	35,000
Net Income available for common stockholders	$420,000
Shares of common stock outstanding	200,000 shares
Earnings per share on common stock	$ 2.10

23 ACCOUNTING PRINCIPLES

SELF-TEST

DIRECTIONS: Write your answers (a, b, c, or d; or True or False) on the numbered lines to the right. To check your answers, turn to page **93**.

1. *The going concern assumption requires that*
   a inventory be valued at the proceeds to be realized by forced sale or auction
   b fixed assets be stated at current market value
   c prepaid expenses be treated as assets
   d goodwill purchased be written off

2. *In a period of inflation, which inventory method would be considered conservative by the accountant?*
   a Last in–first out (lifo)
   b First in–first out (fifo)
   c Average cost
   d Standard cost

3. *Consistency in reference to application of accounting principles refers to the fact that*
   a companies in the same industry use identical accounting procedures and methods and are consistent
   b all presented methods and procedures have been utilized
   c income and assets have not been overstated
   d accounting methods and procedures used have been consistently applied from year to year

4. *Several accepted methods of revenue recognition include*
   a fifo, lifo, and weighted average
   b point of sale, installment, and percentage of completion
   c FOB shipping point and FOB destination
   d current, deferred, and long-term

5. *The assumption of the stable monetary unit is violated when*
   a inventory is valued at the lower of cost or market
   b fixed assets are written up above cost
   c accounts receivable are stated at net realizable value
   d purchased goodwill is recorded

6. A basic accounting assumption is the stability of the monetary unit.

7. The "going concern" concept has an impact upon the valuation of inventory.

8. Inventories are valued at the lower of cost or market.

9. In selecting among several possible treatments of an item, the accountant would tend to select the one that results in the lower net income.

10. Materiality is not considered in the application of accounting principles.

11. Comparability and consistency requirements refer to financial statements of companies within the same industry.

12. The accounting profession prohibits management from changing the method of handling an item.

13. Many areas of accounting are judgmental in nature, requiring the accountant to obtain objective evidence upon which to base his decision.

1 ______
2 ______
3 ______
4 ______
5 ______
6 ______
7 ______
8 ______
9 ______
10 ______
11 ______
12 ______
13 ______

BASIC FACTS

Development of Accounting Principles. It became apparent that with the complexities of business enterprises and the involvement of such outside parties as shareholders, a framework of concepts and accounting principles had to be developed. The accounting profession, recognizing the man-made nature of accounting law, realized that there would have to be general acceptance before an accounting theory could achieve status as a *principle*. The American Institute of Certified Public Accountants has issued various pronouncements laying down such guide lines. There are various outside factors which are constantly acting to influence accounting principles. Government regulations, business practices and the needs of statement readers keep accounting principles in a constantly evolving state.

Accounting Assumptions. Two basic assumptions in accounting are (1) *the going concern assumption*; and (2) *the stability of the monetary unit assumption*. The life of the corporation is usually perpetual and it is assumed that the entity will continue in business for an indefinite period. The going concern concept, therefore, requires treatment of items in the following manner:

(a) Inventory is valued at lower of cost or market, without regard to the proceeds that would be realized by a forced sale or auction.

(b) Fixed assets are systematically depreciated, where applicable, without referring to market or liquidation values.

(c) Prepaid expenses are treated as assets even though they would have little, if any, recovery values in the event the entity ceased doing business.

Accounting assumes a stable monetary unit, the dollar, in spite of the instability of its purchasing power. For accounting purposes, a 1939 dollar is identical with a current dollar. This assumption has considerable impact in the inventory and fixed assets areas. Many accountants believe that supplemental financial statements should be supplied, providing current values by adjusting for price-level changes.

Principles of Accounting Practice. In the application of principles to a particular accounting area or problem, the following guidelines have evolved:

Conservatism. Philosophically, the accountant is conservative in nature. In selection among various possible treatments, there is a tendency to favor the one that results in the lower net income or asset valuation. The accountant will anticipate all losses and recognize profits only when realized. In recent years the tendency for over-conservatism by accountants has been criticized; conservatism should not be considered the primary basis in selecting among several possible alternatives.

Materiality. In the application of generally accepted accounting principles, the relative importance must be considered as to treatment of the item and disclosure in the financial statements. The size of the amount should be considered in relation to such factors as net income and total assets.

Consistency. Generally accepted accounting principles often allow for more than a single "correct" method of handling an item. If the various acceptable alternatives are used in different accounting periods at the whim of management, certain undesirable results will occur. The statement reader will not be able to ascertain trends, either as to income or financial position, because of the lack of comparability with prior statements. Management will be granted a measure of control over the amount of reported income. It is imperative, therefore, that the accounting methods selected be applied consistently from year to year.

The accounting method used should be the one that will most fairly reflect financial position and the results of operations. When business conditions change, it may be advisable to change the method of accounting. When this occurs, there must be full and adequate disclosure of the nature of the change. The financial statements should disclose the change and state the effect of the change on net income.

Objectivity. Many areas of accounting are judgmental in nature, such as the determination of the allowance for bad debts and determining "market" as related to inventory valuation at the lower of cost or market. In these situations the accountant obtains objective evidence upon which to base his decision.

Revenues. The problem of revenue recognition has been bothersome to the accounting profession. At what point of time is the revenue realized? Several accepted methods are the following:

Point of Sale. Traditionally, revenue is realized at the time title passes. At this point in time, there has been an exchange of assets resulting in the realization of profit. The measurement of the profit can be determined from the sales price received. A legal claim has been granted the seller against the buyer for performance (i.e., payment of the sales price).

Installment Method. In the retail trade, sales are often made on an installment plan. The purchaser makes a down payment against the purchase price and pays the balance in monthly installments over a period of time–6 months, 12 months, 24 months, etc. The installment sale may be treated in the same manner as any sale, with recognition of revenue at the point of sale. A less acceptable alternative is income recogni-

(Continued on page 94)

EXPLANATIONS

1. *The going concern assumption requires* that prepaid expenses be treated as assets. The going concern concept implies that the corporation's life is unlimited. Therefore, prepaid expenses are treated as assets since they will be consumed and generate revenue in the course of normal operations. The other answers imply that the corporation has a limited life.

2. *In a period of inflation, last in–first out (lifo) would be considered a conservative inventory method by the accountant.* Conservatism to the accountant is the selection among various acceptable treatments of the one that results in the lowest net income or asset valuation. In a period of inflation the last in-first out (lifo) method results in a lower ending inventory, higher cost of goods sold and lower net income.

3. *Consistency in reference to application of accounting principles refers to the fact that* accounting methods and procedures used have been consistently applied from year to year. The concept of consistency does not prohibit changes where business conditions dictate the advisability of such modification.

4. *Several accepted methods of revenue recognition include* point of sale, installment, and percentage of completion, as well as point of production, and percentage of services rendered. The other terms do not refer to revenue recognition methods.

5. *The assumption of the stable monetary unit is violated when* fixed assets are written up above cost. The assumption is that, for accounting purposes, a 1939 dollar is identical with a current dollar. Fixed assets are recorded at their original cost less accumulated depreciation and should not be written up.

6. *A basic accounting assumption is the stability of the monetary unit.* Although it is acknowledged by accountants that the dollar is an unstable limit of measurement, no recognition is given to the monetary fluctuations in the financial statements.

7. *The "going concern" concept has an impact upon the valuation* of inventory. If not for this assumption, inventory would have to be valued at liquidation value, instead of the lower of cost or market principle actually used.

8. *Inventories are valued at the lower of cost or market.* The going concern concept and the concept of conservatism are the basis for this accounting principle.

9. *In selecting among several possible treatments of an item, the accountant would tend to select the one that results in the lower net income.* The accountant has always tended to be conservative in the treatment of financial transactions.

10. *Materiality* is *considered in the application of accounting principles.* Items of little or no importance can be handled in the most expeditious manner, without regard to accounting principles.

11. *Comparability and consistency requirements do not refer to financial statements of companies within the same industry.* The concepts refer to successive financial statements of a single entity. Their aim is to enable the statement reader to identify trends within the operation of the business.

12. *The accounting profession does* not *prohibit management from changing accounting methods.* Any changes, however, must be to another *accepted* accounting method and the effect of the change must be reported in the financial statements.

13. *Many areas of accounting are judgmental in nature, requiring the accountant to obtain objective evidence upon which to base his decision.* Sales and purchase invoices and bank statements are examples of objective and verifiable documentary evidence.

Answers

c	1
a	2
d	3
b	4
b	5
T	6
T	7
T	8
T	9
F	10
F	11
F	12
T	13

tion under the installment method. In this instance income is realized concurrently with the receipt of cash. Each receipt of cash consists of a return of cost and a portion of the profit on the sale.

Percentage of Contract Completion. In the heavy construction industry, completion of a particular project may involve several years. The serious problem is whether the net income should be recognized only in the year in which the contract is completed. It is considered generally acceptable to reflect revenue over the period of the contract based on the percentage of completion. The related costs are reflected in the period the revenue is recognized, i.e., matching costs against revenues. There is some degree of uncertainty involved in this method.

Others. These include point of production and percentage of services rendered which are considered acceptable under given conditions.

24 INCOME TAXES

SELF-TEST

DIRECTIONS: For questions 1–9 write your answers (T or F) on the numbered lines to the right. To check your answers, turn to page 97.

1. The federal income tax is a progressive tax.

2. Individuals most often employ the accrual method of accounting for tax purposes.

3. Married individuals are taxed at lower rates than single persons.

4. The doctrine of constructive receipt causes income to be taxed when received.

5. There are only two acceptable methods of accounting for tax purposes—the cash method and the accrual method.

6. The normal deduction allowed for personal exemptions for each individual is $1,000.

7. The standard deduction can never exceed $1,000.

8. A married couple, both under 65 years of age, with three children and an adjusted gross income of $6,000 can claim a standard deduction of $700.

9. Partnerships are taxed at lower rates than corporations but higher than individuals.

10. John Smith, a 45 year old engineer, earned $18,000 last year. His wife, Mary, 43 years old, had no income of her own. They have two children, one of whom lives at college. Both children receive all of their support from their parents. The Smiths provide the full support of Harry Allen, Mrs. Smith's 70 year old father. During the year the Smiths paid $840 in real estate taxes, $240 in contributions, mortgage interest of $1,150 and state income taxes of $350. Mr. Smith also gave a wedding gift of $500 to his nephew. *Compute the taxable income of John and Mary Smith.*

To check your answer, turn to page 97.

1 ______
2 ______
3 ______
4 ______
5 ______
6 ______
7 ______
8 ______
9 ______

BASIC FACTS

Nature of Taxes. The federal income tax became an economic fact of life in 1913, when the Sixteenth Amendment to the Constitution gave Congress the right to levy taxes on income. To individuals, and to some extent to the corporation, the income tax is a *progressive* tax, which means that as the taxable base increases, the tax rate becomes progressively greater. Current rates for individuals run to a high of 70% of taxable income. Corporations are taxed at a maximum of 48%.

The tax law is based on the principle of self-assessment; taxable income is computed by the *taxpayer*, the tax rate is applied, and the tax due is paid to the government. Audit of returns by the Internal Revenue Service accounts for approximately 3% of the total revenue collected; the remaining 97% is received through voluntary compliance with the tax laws.

Cash and Accrual Basis. Accounting is not an exact science; the choice of an accounting method and the application of variously acceptable accounting principles will result in differing amounts of reportable taxable income. The Internal Revenue Code allows the taxpayer to choose the method of accounting that he wishes to use in the computation of taxable income. The basic methods are the *cash basis* and the *accrual basis*, although hybrid methods are also acceptable. The only requirement is that the accounting method chosen result in a fair determination of taxable income.

Cash Basis Accounting is used by most individuals and by some business entities. Amounts are included in income when actually received, deductions are allowed to reduce income only when paid. There are several exceptions to the strict application of the above rule: (1) The doctrine of *constructive receipt* requires that an item be included in income when the taxpayer has such control that he can determine when he will actually take receipt. (2) Payments made for the acquisition of assets with a useful life of more than one year cannot be deducted in the year paid. The deduction must be pro-rated over the life of the asset. (3) Prepayments of expenses cannot be deducted in the year of payment; the deduction must wait until the year the expense is incurred.

Accrual Basis Accounting recognizes income when it is realized and expenses when incurred. It is not necessary that cash be received or disbursed. Most businesses, other than service businesses, elect to use the accrual method. Where inventories are a material factor, the government requires that the accrual method be used.

Classes of Taxpayers. Individuals, estates, trusts, and corporations are all subject to taxation under the Internal Revenue Code. Partnerships are not consid-

(*Continued on page 98*)

EXPLANATIONS

1. *The federal income tax is a progressive tax,* which means that as the taxable base increases the tax rate becomes progressively greater. Individual rates range from 14% to 70%.

2. *Individuals do* not *often employ the accrual method of accounting for tax purposes.* The cash basis method of accounting is usually used by individuals. The accrual method is most often employed by business enterprises.

3. *Married individuals are taxed at lower rates than single persons.* There are three different rate structures in the Internal Revenue Code. Single taxpayers pay the highest rates; married taxpayers pay the lowest; the head of the household category is in the middle.

4. *The doctrine of constructive receipt* does not *cause income to be taxed when received.* The doctrine of constructive receipt causes income to be taxed when it comes under the control of the taxpayer. It is not necessary that the money or property representing the income be in the taxpayer's possession.

5. *There are* more than two *acceptable methods of accounting for tax purposes.* The Internal Revenue Code permits hybrid methods of accounting for tax reporting. The only requisites are that there be consistency of application and that the method used results in a fair determination of income.

6. *The normal deduction allowed for personal exemptions for each individual is* not *$1,000;* the deduction for personal exemptions is set at $600.

7. *The standard deduction can never exceed $1,000.* The standard deduction is 10% of the adjusted gross income or $300 plus $100 for each personal exemption after the first, whichever is greater. There is an overall limitation of $1,000.

8. *A married couple, both under 65 years of age, with three children and an adjusted gross income of $6,000 can claim a standard deduction of $700.* The 10% standard deduction would allow for a $600 standard deduction. The minimum standard deduction would be $700; $300 for the first exemption and $100 for each additional exemption.

9. *Partnerships are* not *taxed at lower rates than corporations but higher than individuals.* Partnerships are not taxable entities and pay no income tax. The partnership files a tax return, but it is for informational purposes only.

Answers

T	1
F	2
T	3
F	4
F	5
F	6
T	7
T	8
F	9

10.

Gross income		$18,000
Deductions to arrive at adjusted gross income		0
Adjusted gross income		$18,000
Deductions from adjusted gross income:		
Contributions	$ 240	
Real estate taxes	840	
State income taxes	350	
Mortgage interest	1,150	2,580
Balance		15,420
Personal exemptions (5 × $600)		3,000
Taxable income		$12,420

Note: The wedding gift is not deductible.

ered to be entities separate from the individual partners. Each partner reports his proportionate share of partnership income or loss on his personal tax return. Individuals who are married or who qualify as a head of a household are subject to different tax rates than single individuals. In all cases, the rates are progressive but the schedule of rates for head of household is less steep than for unmarried individuals. Married persons are taxed at the lowest rates of all the groups. Corporations generally pay tax at the rate of 22% on the first $25,000 of taxable income. Thereafter the rate is a constant 48%.

Concepts of Tax Law

Individuals The starting point for the computation of taxable income is *gross income.* Gross income includes all items of income not excluded by law. If an item of income is to escape taxation, the Internal Revenue Code must specifically provide for the exclusion.

An individual is allowed certain deductions from his gross income, to arrive at *adjusted gross income.* These deductions are limited to the following:

1. All ordinary and necessary expenses incurred in carrying on a business or profession.
2. Certain expenses incurred by an employee in connection with his employment.
3. Expenses incurred in connection with rent and royalty income.
4. Losses from sale or exchange of property acquired for the production of income.
5. The long-term capital gain deduction. This allows for a deduction of 50% of taxable net long-term capital gain.

After the adjusted gross income is determined, an individual has two options. He may itemize his deductions or take a standard deduction. There are two methods of computing the standard deduction. The *first* allows a deduction to the extent of 10% of the adjusted gross income, with a maximum of $1,000. The *second* method allows a deduction of $300 plus $100 for each personal exemption after the first. Married taxpayers not filing joint returns are limited to a $500 maximum under the first method and a $200 base deduction instead of $300 under the second method.

Itemized deductions are limited to the following areas: medical expenses, contributions, interest, taxes, expenses necessary for the production of income, and casualty losses. In addition to these deductions *from* adjusted gross income, there is allowed a deduction for personal exemptions. Each individual is allowed a deduction of $600. Additional $600 exemptions are allowed for blindness and for being over 65 years of age. A taxpayer is allowed to claim a personal exemption for himself, his wife (if a joint return is filed) and all individuals he can claim as dependents.

After the deductions and personal exemptions are subtracted from adjusted gross income, the balance remaining is the taxable income. The tax due is computed by consulting the appropriate rate table and applying the rates indicated.

Corporations. The computation of corporate taxable income is a two step procedure. Gross income is determined and all deductions are subtracted from this total in order to arrive at taxable income. Unlike individual returns, there is no need to arrive at an intermediary "adjusted gross income" nor is there any personal exemption allowed the corporation.

ILLUSTRATIONS AND EXAMPLES

Concepts of Tax Law

Basic Tax Computation for Individuals:

Gross income	$20,000
Less: deductions to arrive at adjusted gross income (i.e. employee transportation expense)	560
Adjusted gross income	19,440
Less: itemized deductions or standard deductions	1,530
personal exemptions (4 × $600)	2,400
Total deductions	3,930
Taxable income	$15,510

Tax computed on taxable income is based on the applicable tax table (single, married, or head of household)

Basic Tax Computation for Corporations:

Gross income	$100,000
Deductions (expenses)	42,000
Taxable income	$ 58,000
Normal tax, 22% of $58,000	$ 12,760
Surtax, 26% of ($58,000–$25,000)	8,580
Total income tax	$ 21,340

Answers to questions 2 and 3, Chapter 21.

2.

FORMAT I

MARC RICHARDS & COMPANY
Statement of Source and Application of Funds
Year Ended December 31, 19__

Source of Funds			
Operations			
Net income for the year		$5,500	
Add: non-cash expenses			
Depreciation of furniture and equipment	$2,370		
Loss on sale of furniture	250	2,620	
From operations			$ 8,120
Sale of capital stock			3,500
Sale of furniture			250
Total sources of funds			$11,870
Application of Funds			
Purchase of equipment		$7,400	
Declaration of dividends		800	
Total application of funds			8,200
Increase in working capital			$3,670

FORMAT II

MARC RICHARDS & COMPANY
Statement of Source and Application of Funds
Year Ended December 31, 19__

Source of Funds		
Sales	$41,000	
Sale of capital stock	3,500	
Sale of furniture	250	
Total sources of funds		$44,750
Application of Funds		
Cost of goods sold	$22,730	
Selling and administrative expenses	8,500	
Provision for bad debts	150	
Provision for federal income taxes	1,500	
Purchase of equipment	7,400	
Declaration of dividends	800	
Total application of funds		41,080
Increase in working capital		$3,670

3. *Case A*	Capital stock (subsidiary)	60,000	
	Retained earnings (subsidiary)	20,000	
	Investment		80,000
Case B	Capital stock (subsidiary)	48,000	
	Retained earnings (subsidiary)	16,000	
	Investment		64,000
Case C	Capital stock (subsidiary)	54,000	
	Retained earnings (deficit)–Subsidiary		9,000
	Investment		45,000
Case D	Capital stock (subsidiary)	54,000	
	Retained earnings (deficit)–Subsidiary		9,000
	Excess of net assets acquired over cost of subsidiary stock		5,000
	Investment		40,000
Case E	Capital stock (subsidiary)	48,000	
	Retained earnings (subsidiary)	32,000	
	Excess of cost of subsidiary stock over net assets acquired	15,000	
	Investment		95,000

FINAL EXAMINATION PART I

DIRECTIONS: Write your answer (a, b, c, or d; or T or F) on the numbered lines in the margins. To check your answers, turn to pages **104** and **105**. Study the explanations for any questions you missed.

1 ________
2 ________
3 ________
4 ________
5 ________
6 ________
7 ________
8 ________
9 ________
10 ________
11 ________
12 ________
13 ________
14 ________

1. *The basis of accounting for inventories is*
   - a market value
   - b last in, first out
   - c cost
   - d first in, first out

2. *The following item is not properly includible in inventory*
   - a raw materials
   - b machinery maintenance supplies
   - c sales commissions
   - d freight in

3. *The name for an entry putting an unrecorded cost on the books is*
   - a accrual
   - b deferral
   - c prepayment
   - d closing

4. *The intangible not subject to amortization is*
   - a leasehold cost
   - b patent cost
   - c goodwill cost
   - d copyright costs

5. *The following characteristics are attributable to partnerships*
   - a limited liability, limited life, separate legal entity
   - b unlimited liability, limited life, no separate legal entity
   - c limited liability, limited life, separate legal entity
   - d limited liability, unlimited life, no separate legal entity

Answer True or False to questions 6–10.

6. *Cash, restricted to use in the liquidation of long term debt, is properly presented as a current asset.*

7. *Unpaid wages are a contingent liability.*

8. *When an impress petty cash system is used, the petty cash account is debited* only *when the fund is replenished.*

9. *The general ledger is the basic book of original entry.*

10. *Where "allowance for doubtful accounts" appears on a company's balance sheet, the advance provision method of recording bad debts is being used.*

11. If Brown purchases Smith's interest in the partnership Smith & Jones
   - a the partnership assets must be revalued
   - b there will be an increase in the amount of partnership assets
   - c the price paid will not be reflected on the books of account
   - d goodwill may be recognized to the incoming partner

12. Jones invests $50,000 for a 25% interest in a partnership. The two old partners have capital balances totaling $100,000. Each old partner will be credited for partnership goodwill in the amount of
   - a $20,000
   - b $50,000
   - c $30,000
   - d $25,000

13. X, Y and Z are partners sharing profits equally. Partners X and Y have capital accounts of $20,000 and $15,000 respectively. Partner Z, who is personally insolvent, has a deficit balance of $5,000. The partnership assets are sold at a $3,000 loss and the business is liquidated. Partner X will receive cash of
   - a $20,000
   - b $16,000
   - c $19,000
   - d $15,000

14. *Which of the following asset groupings contains only current assets*
   - a cash, accounts receivable, furniture and fixtures
   - b inventory, prepaid expenses, trade acceptances receivable
   - c land, notes receivable, goodwill
   - d marketable securities, patents, copyrights

15. *The following statement does not apply to fixed assets:*
    a they have a useful life of more than one year
    b they must be depreciated or amortized
    c they are intended for use in the operations of the business
    d they are subject to disposal by sale, trade, or abandonment

16. On November 29 the X Company recorded and sent a certified check for $4,600 to a creditor. This check was not deposited by the creditor until December 5. On the Company's bank reconciliation at the end of November, this item should be
    a deducted from the balance shown on the November 30 bank statement
    b deducted from the cash balance shown on X Company's books
    c added to the bank balance shown on the November 30 bank statement
    d ignored, since the books and the bank statement are in agreement

17. *Richards Company has a balance of $25,000 in its notes receivable account and a balance of $6000 in its notes receivable discounted account. The company has*
    a an asset of $31,000 and a contingent liability of $6,000
    b an asset of $25,000 and a contingent liability of $6,000
    c an asset of $19,000 and a contingent liability of $6,000
    d an asset of $25,000 and a liability of $6,000

18. *When the sum-of-years digits method of accounting is used*
    a depreciation expense will be higher in years of high production, lower in years of low production
    b depreciation expense will be constant for each accounting period
    c depreciation expense will decline progressively in succeeding accounting periods
    d depreciation expense will increase progressively in succeeding accounting periods

19. *Company x has inadvertantly overstated its ending inventory by $10,000. This will*
    a increase the income of the succeeding period by $10,000
    b decrease the income of the succeeding period by $10,000
    c decrease the income of the current period by $10,000
    d have no effect on the income of the succeeding year

20. At January 1, 19___ Y Company had an allowance for bad debts of $1,000. During the year a monthly provision of 1% of sales was made for uncollectible accounts. Sales for the year were $360,000. Accounts of $2,300 were written off, of which $400 were collected later in the year. At the year end
    a allowance for bad debts will have a $2,700 credit balance
    b bad debt expense will have a debit balance of $1,900
    c allowance for bad debts will have a $2,300 credit balance
    d bad debt expense will have a debit balance of $3,200

15 ________
16 ________
17 ________
18 ________
19 ________
20 ________

Answers

c	1
c	2
d	3
c	4
b	5
F	6
F	7
F	8
F	9
T	10
c	11
d	12
b	13
b	14

EXPLANATIONS

1. The basis of accounting for inventories is cost, on the principle that accounting is primarily based on cost. Last in, first out and first in, first out are simply assumptions as to the flow of costs.

2. An item not properly includible in inventory is sales commissions. The other items are part of the cost of manufacturing the tangible property and are therefore inventoriable.

3. The name for an entry putting an unrecorded cost on the books is an accrual.

4. The intangible not subject to amortization is goodwill. Only those intangibles with a limited life are properly amortizable. Goodwill, not having a limited useful life, is carried on the books for the entire life of the entity.

5. Characteristics attributable to partnerships include unlimited liability, limited life, and the absence of a separate legal entity.

6. Cash, restricted to use in the liquidation of long term debt, *is not* properly presented as a current asset. It is not available for the payment of current liabilities, nor can it enter the circular flow of capital from cash to inventory to receivables to cash.

7. Unpaid wages are *not* a contingent liability, they are an actual liability. To be classified as a contingent liability, there must be a degree of uncertainty concerning whether or not the liability will develop. This "improbability factor" does not exist with unpaid wages.

8. When an imprest petty cash system is used, the petty cash account is *not* debited when the fund is replenished. The account is debited only when the fund is established. When the fund is replenished, the debit is to the various expense accounts.

9. The general ledger is *not* the basic book of original entry. A ledger is not a book of original entry. The general journal is the basic book of original entry.

10. Where "allowance for doubtful accounts" appears on a company's balance sheet, the advance provision method of recording bad debts is being used. An estimate of the loss from uncollectible accounts is recorded on the books.

11. When a partnership interest is purchased, the transaction is between the incoming and outgoing partners. The partnership books give effect to the transaction only by recording a transfer of the old partner's capital account to the new partner.

12. Each partner will be credited with $25,000 of goodwill, computed as follows:

Investment by Jones for 25% interest		$50,000
Indicated value of partnership ($50,000 × 4)		$200,000
Equity of old partners	$100,000	
Additional investment	50,000	
Equity before recording goodwill		150,000
Partnership goodwill		$ 50,000
Goodwill attributable to each old partner (50% each)		$ 25,000

13. Partner X will receive a cash distribution of $16,000, computed as follows:

	(In Thousands)			
	X	*Y*	*Z*	*Total*
Capital account balance	20	15	(5)	30
Loss on sale of assets	(1)	(1)	(1)	(3)
Balance after loss	19	14	(6)	27
Elimination of deficit	(3)	(3)	6	
Cash distribution	16	11	–	27

14. The asset group that contains only current assets is inventory, prepaid expenses, and trade acceptances receivable. Furniture and fixtures and land are classified as fixed assets; goodwill, patents, and copyrights are intangibles.

15. It is not a true statement that fixed assets must be depreciated or amortized. Land, which does not lose its usefulness with the passage of time, is a fixed asset not subject to depreciation or amortization.

16. The Company's bank reconciliation at the end of November will not give effect to the outstanding certified check, since the bank statement and the books of account are in agreement. Certified checks are deducted from the drawer's account at the time of certification. When preparing the bank reconciliation, certified checks must be excluded from the outstanding checks.

17. The Company has an asset of $19,000 and a contingent liability of $6,000. The notes receivable discounted is a contingent liability of the endorser. It does not become an actual liability until the maker defaults at maturity. When the notes were discounted, the Company gave up ownership of $6,000 worth of notes for cash. The asset value of the notes must be reduced by the discounted amount.

18. When the sum-of-years digits method of accounting is used, depreciation expense will decline progressively in succeeding accounting periods. This is one of the most widely used accelerated depreciation methods in which a declining rate is applied to the cost of the asset.

19. Company X, in overstating its ending inventory by $10,000, will decrease the income of the succeeding period by $10,000. The overstatement of the ending inventory will cause a similar overstatement in the beginning inventory of the following period. This opening inventory is a charge against income; therefore an overstatement of this figure will decrease income.

20. At the end of the year, the allowance for bad debts will have a credit balance of $2,700, computed as follows:

Balance in account- Jan. 1, 19--	$1,000
Add: Provision for year-1% of annual sales	3,600
: Recovery of amounts written off	400
	$5,000
Deduct: Uncollectible accounts written off	2,300
Balance in account- Dec. 31, 19--	$2,700

Answer	No.
b	15
d	16
c	17
c	18
b	19
a	20

FINAL EXAMINATION, PART II

DIRECTIONS: Write your answer (a, b, c, or d; or T or F) on the numbered lines in the margins. To check your answers, turn to pages **108** and **109**. Study the explanations for any questions you missed.

1 ________
2 ________
3 ________
4 ________
5 ________
6 ________
7 ________
8 ________
9 ________
10 ________
11 ________
12 ________
13 ________

1. *The following item does not give rise to an actual liability*
   - a declaration of a dividend by a corporation
   - b an assessment by federal tax authorities
   - c a contested claim of patent infringement
   - d receipt of payment prior to rendering services

2. *Corporation X has 200,000 shares of authorized common stock, of which 150,000 shares are outstanding. At December 31, the capital section shows the following:*

Capital stock	$300,000
Capital surplus	$150,000
Retained earnings	$750,000

The book value of one share of common stock is:
   - a $8.00
   - b $6.00
   - c $7.00
   - d $3.00

3. *Partnerships are taxed at the same rates as*
   - a individuals
   - b corporations
   - c estates and trusts
   - d none of the above

4. *In classifying expenses as either fixed or variable, depreciation expense*
   - a is classified as a variable expense
   - b is classified as a fixed expense
   - c may be classified as either fixed or variable, depending on the basis for computing depreciation
   - d may be classified as either fixed or variable, depending on basis for allocating sales

Corporation A authorized a 10 year bond issue of $4,000,000 on October 1, 1967. The bonds carry interest of 6%, payable April 1 and October 1. The entire bond issue was sold on December 1, 1967 and the company received $4,276,000.

5. *What was the issue price of the bonds?*
   - a $106.40
   - b $125.60
   - c $105.90
   - d $100.00

6. *The interest expense to the corporation in 1967 was*
   - a $60,000
   - b $20,000
   - c $21,280
   - d $18,000

Answer True or False to questions 7–12.

7. In using the contribution margin method to report departmental operations, only the indirect expenses are allocated to the various departments.

8. When a corporation "splits its stock," it is motivated by the desire to increase its working capital.

9. A consolidated balance sheet reports the financial condition of an economic unit.

10. The current ratio, equity ratio and the acid test (quick ratio) all are used to measure liquidity.

11. The procedure known as direct costing requires the inclusion of direct material, direct labor and fixed overhead as product costs.

12. Underapplied manufacturing overhead may be added to the cost of goods sold.

13. Corporation X reacquires 100 shares of its common stock for $14,000. These shares have a par value of $100 and were originally sold for $25. above par. As a result of this acquisition, the corporation:
   - a has reduced its shareholders' equity by $10,000
   - b has reduced its shareholders' equity by $14,000
   - c has increased its shareholders' equity by $2,500
   - d has increased its shareholders' equity by $14,000

14. *The shareholders' equity section includes the following accounts:*

Preferred 6% stock, $25 par value; 20,000 shares authorized, issued and outstanding	500,000
Common stock, $10 par value; 250,000 shares authorized, 200,000 issued (including 20,000 shares in the treasury)	2,000,000

The Board of Directors has decided to distribute earnings in the amount of $750,000. This will result in a dividend on each share of common stock of
a $3.75
b $4.167
c $3.00
d $4.00

15. *A corporation has total assets of $800,000 and contributed capital of $200,000. The total of the shareholders' equity is 30% of the total assets. From this information it can be determined that the corporation has*
a retained earnings of $40,000
b liabilities of $600,000
c a deficit of $140,000
d liabilities of $140,000

16. *On January 1, Corporation P acquired 90% of the stock of Corporation S for $270,000. At that date, the subsidiary's equity section showed:*

Capital stock	$200,000
Retained earnings	$ 80,000
Total stockholders equity	$280,000

The investment account elimination entry will include
a a debit to "excess cost of subsidiary over net assets acquired" of $18,000
b a credit to "excess of net assets acquired over cost of subsidiary stock" of $10,000
c a debit to "excess cost of subsidiary over net assets acquired" of $10,000
d a credit to capital surplus of $18,000

17. Which of the following best describes the book value of a share of stock?
a The amount at which the stock would sell on the open market if sold by a willing and informed buyer to a willing and informed seller.
b The amount which the owner of one share of stock would receive if his share was redeemed at its stated value.
c The amount which the owner of one share of stock would receive on liquidation if the assets were sold at their book value and all liabilities were paid.
d. An amount computed by dividing the total assets as shown on the books by the number of shares outstanding.

18. The following journal entry appears on the books of Adams Co.

Bonds Payable	50,000	
Premium on Bonds	1,000	
Cash		48,000
Gain on Retirement		3,000

This entry records the following:
a the retirement of $50,000 of bonds at 98
b the retirement of $47,000 of bonds at par
c the retirement of $50,000 of bonds at par
d the retirement of $50,000 of bonds at 96

Answer True or False to questions 19 and 20.

19. A bond sinking fund is a restricted cash account that must be used exclusively to pay the bondholders at maturity.

20. A stock dividend is not considered to be income to the recipient.

14 ______
15 ______
16 ______
17 ______
18 ______
19 ______
20 ______

Answers

c	1
a	2
d	3
c	4
c	5
d	6
F	7
F	8
T	9
F	10
F	11
T	12
b	13

EXPLANATIONS

1. A contested claim of patent infringement does not give rise to an actual liability. There is a degree of uncertainty connected with a contested claim which results in its being classified as a contingent liability. Until a *possible* obligation becomes a *probable* obligation, it is a contingent rather than actual liability.

2. The book value of one share of common stock is \$8.00. The book value is computed by dividing the shareholders' equity by the number of outstanding shares. Corporation X has shareholders' equity of \$1,200,000 and 150,000 outstanding shares, resulting in an \$8.00 book value.

3. Partnerships, unlike corporations, estates, trusts, and individuals, are not taxable entities. Their income is not subject to tax. Instead, the individual partners pay tax on their distributive share of the partnership income.

4. Depreciation expense may be classified as either fixed or variable, depending on the basis for computing the expense. When computed on the unit of production basis, it is a variable expense. The other common depreciation methods do not vary with production and will therefore result in a fixed expense.

5. The issue price of the bonds was \$105.90. The price received for the bonds was \$4,236,000; the additional \$40,000 received was to adjust for the fact that the bonds were sold between interest dates. Dividing the amount received for the bonds by the par or face amount gives an issue price of \$105.90.

6. The interest expense to the corporation was \$18,000. The bond premium of \$236,000 must be amortized over the life of the bonds, reducing the interest expense. The corporation paid interest of \$20,000 for the month of December. This must be reduced by \$2,000, one month's amortization of the bond premium.

(December 1, 1967 to October 1, 1977 = 118 months.
\$236,000 ÷ 118 = \$2,000 per month.)

7. Indirect expenses are not allocated to departments under the contribution margin method of reporting income. Only *direct* departmental expenses are deducted from departmental revenues; the result is the department's contribution to the indirect expenses of the business.

8. When a corporation splits its stock it is not motivated by the desire to increase its working capital. The sole reason for splitting the stock is to reduce the unit market price of the shares. Its function is to aid the marketability of the shares.

9. The consolidated balance sheet reports the financial condition of an *economic* entity. The parent corporation and its subsidiary companies do not, however, constitute a *legal* entity.

10. The equity ratio is not used as a measure of liquidity. It measures the equity of the shareholders against the claims of the corporation's creditors.

11. Direct costing does not allow the inclusion of fixed overhead as a product cost. Product costs are limited to direct material, direct labor, and variable overhead. Fixed overhead is a period cost.

12. Underapplied manufacturing overhead may be added to the cost of goods sold. Other options are: (a) to treat the variance as a period cost or (b) to allocate it between inventory and cost of goods sold.

13. The corporation has reduced its shareholders' equity by \$14,000. When a corporation reacquires its own shares, it is not acquiring an asset. The corporation is returning a portion of its capital. The reduction in shareholders' equity is the total amount paid in purchasing the treasury shares.

14\. There will be $4.00 dividend on each share of common stock.

Earnings to be distributed	$750,000
Payment on preferred shares	30,000
Remainder-to common stock	$720,000
Outstanding common shares (200,000–20,000)	180,000
Dividend on each share of common	$4.00

15\. The corporation has retained earnings of $40,000. The following computations will prove this answer.

I	Assets	$800,000
	Capital (30% × $800,000)	240,000
	Liabilities	$560,000
II	Total capital	$240,000
	Contributed capital	200,000
	Retained earnings	$ 40,000

16\. The investment account elimination will include a debit to "excess cost of subsidiary over net assets acquired" of $18,000. The parent company paid $270,000 for $252,000 of the subsidiary's equity (90% × $280,000). The $18,000 difference is set up on the elimination of the investment account.

17\. Book value of a share of stock can be described as the amount which the owner of one share would receive on liquidation, if the assets were sold at their book value and all liabilities were paid. A stock's stated or fair market value is in no way related to book value. Assets cannot be used as a basis for computing book value until a reduction has been made for all recorded liabilities.

18\. The journal entry records the retirement of $50,000 of bonds at 96. Bonds are quoted at a price per $100 of face value. By dividing the face amount of the bonds ($50,000) into the cash received ($48,000) the quoted price of 96 is obtained.

19\. A bond sinking fund is a restricted cash account that must be used exclusively to pay the bondholders at maturity. The cash is often deposited with a trustee, who maintains control over the fund until the bond issue matures.

20\. A stock dividend is not considered to be income to the recipient. There is no change in the shareholder's proportional interest in the equity of the corporation. The only change is in the number of shares evidencing this interest.

Answers

d	14
a	15
a	16
c	17
d	18
T	19
T	20

DICTIONARY-INDEX

Capital expenditures: those items which are properly charged to an asset account. They include the acquisition cost of a new asset, the invoice cost, transportation, and installation charges, 40

Capital stock: units evidencing ownership of a corporation. The two major classes of stock are common and preferred, 1, 52

Capitalization of a corporation: term used by investment analysts to indicate the total capital of a corporation plus the par value of any outstanding bonds, 90

Capitalized: charged to an asset account. *See* Capital expenditure.

Cash: any medium of exchange that can be deposited in a bank for immediate credit to the depositor's account, such as checks, money orders, and demand and time deposits, 24

Cash basis accounting: accounting method whereby income is credited when received and expenses charged when paid. Transactions of a non-cash nature are generally not recorded, and an accurate picture of income is not presented, 8, 96

Cash disbursements journal: a book of original entry used to record transactions made by check, 12, 16

Cash dividend: distributions of earnings paid in cash, 60

Cash payments journal: *see* Cash Disbursements Journal.

Cash receipts journal: a book of original entry used to record transactions involving cash receipts, 12, 16

Centralized accounting: refers to branch accounting method where the branch does not maintain a separate set of books. Its activities are incorporated in the journals and ledgers of the home office, 72

Check register: a simplified version of the cash disbursements journal, used in the voucher system, 70

Closing entries: journal entries prepared at the end of an accounting period to close out revenue, expense, and temporary capital accounts, 10

Common size statements: statements prepared using percentages rather than dollar amounts, 88

Common stock: grants to the owner all rights normally accompanying ownership. If a corporation has only one class of stock it is termed common. Where a second or preferred class of stock exists certain rights of the common shareholders will be subordinated (*see also* Capital Stock), 52

Comparative financial statements: balance sheets or income statements reflecting more than one date of accounting period, prepared for comparison purposes.

Conservatism: an accounting doctrine that calls for providing for all possible losses while anticipating no profits, 92

Consistency: the accounting concept which calls for the constant application of accepted accounting principles from year to year, 92

Consolidated balance sheet: a balance sheet which presents the assets and liabilities of a parent corporation and its subsidiaries as if they were one entity, 84, 86

Consolidated income statement: an income statement which presents the results of operations of a parent corporation and its subsidiaries as if they were one entity, 84, 86

Constructive receipt: an item is included in income when the taxpayer has such control that he can determine when he will actually take receipt, 96

Contingent liability: a potential liability to the corporation. Future events will either result in the elimination of all liability or the creation of a real liability, 66

Contributed capital: the net worth of the corporation reduced by undistributed profits. It consists of capital stock and paid-in capital, 60

Controlling account: a general ledger account equal to the sum of the balances in the individual accounts in the subsidiary ledger.

Convertible bonds: bonds which may be exchanged by the holder for other securities of the issuing corporation, 66

Convertible preferred stock: shares which grant the owner the right to convert the stock into another form of security. Usually convertible into common stock of the company at a fixed rate, 54

Corporation: a legal entity given authority to act by a particular state. A charter is granted and the corporation may then issue capital stock and transact business, 1, 52

Cost: amount expended or liability incurred for goods or services.

Cost accounting: system used to determine the cost of materials, labor and overhead entering into the manufacture of a product for sale, 80

Cost accounting systems: *see* Job Order Cost System and Process Cost System.

Cost of goods sold: the cost of goods manufactured or purchased, adjusted for changes in opening and closing inventory, 22

Coupon bonds: bonds which have interest coupons attached to the bond certificate. Issuer does not maintain ownership files on these bondholders and interest is paid to bearer upon presenting the coupons, 66

Credit: right side of an account.

Cumulative preferred stock: preferred stock which must be paid any dividends in arrears on its shares before common shareholders can receive dividends, 54, 60

Current assets: assets which are expected to be realized in cash or consumed in the normal operating cycle of the business, 20, 88, 90

Current liabilities: liabilities which require the use of current assets or the creation of other current liabilities for their liquidation, 20, 64, 88, 90

Current ratio: current assets divided by current liabilities. It is an indication of an entity's debt-paying ability, 20, 88

Debenture bonds: bonds which grant holders no specific security. Only the general credit of the corporation backs a debenture bond issue, 66

Debit: left side of an account.

Debt financing: Borrowing from banks, use of trade credit and sale of bonds, 64

Decentralized accounting: refers to branch accounting method where the branch maintains a separate set of books, 72

Deferred charge: unexpended portion of an expense already paid, 66

Deferred credit: income recorded on the books of account before it is earned, 66

Departmental operations: company operations organized along department lines. Accounting records must provide information as to department efficiency, 72

Depletion: periodic charges to income for the cost of natural resources. The natural resources are being used up and therefore the cost of the resource is charged to expense, 42

Deposits in transit: deposits made near the end of the month and not reflected on the bank statement, 24, 25

Depreciation: loss of usefulness of fixed assets with the passage of time. Causes of depreciation include wear and tear, inadequacy and obsolescence, 36

Depreciation accounting: the allocation of the cost of a fixed asset over the years of productive use, 36

Depreciation methods: used to determine the depreciation expense for a given accounting period. Factors to be considered include cost, estimated salvage value and estimated life. Methods most commonly used are straight-line, sum of years digits, declining balance and units of production, 36

Direct costing: an accounting concept which includes as product or inventoriable costs only raw materials, direct labor and *variable* factory overhead costs, 76

Direct labor: that portion of the factory labor cost which can be directly identified with a specific manufacturing job or process, 76

Direct materials: *see* Raw Materials.

Discount on capital stock: the difference between the par or stated value of capital stock and the amount received on the issuance of the shares, 56

Discounting the note: 30

Dividend: pro-rata distribution of assets by a corporation to its shareholders. Dividends are declared by formal action of the board of directors, 60

Dividends in arrears: refers to cumulative preferred stock where dividends have been omitted, 54, 60

Dividends payable: liability on part of corporation for dividends declared, 60

Donated treasury stock: shares of capital stock donated to the corporation by the shareholders, 58

Double-entry system: bookkeeping system in which at least two accounts are involved in every transaction. Each entry must have an equality of debits and credits, 4

Earnings per share: computed by dividing the amount of net income available for the common stockholders by the number of shares outstanding, 90

Equity financing: issuance of capital stock, 64

Equity ratio: computed by dividing the stockholders' equity by total assets, indicates the portion of assets supplied by the owners, 90

Equivalent production: number of equivalent whole units manufactured, 82

Expenses: the costs of carrying on a business activity, 2

Factory overhead: all costs of manufacturing other than raw material and direct labor. Included are equipment maintenance, indirect materials, depreciation, heat, indirect labor and special service department costs, 76, 82

Federal income tax: a tax on income imposed by the federal government, 96

Financial statements: principal statements are the balance sheet, income, and funds, 88

Finished goods: goods that have completed the production process and are ready for sale, 80

First In–First Out: assumption as to flow of costs in which costs are charged against revenue in the order in which they were incurred. This method reflects the ending inventory at the current value, as indicated by the most recent purchase, 32

Fixed assets: assets with a useful life extending beyond the current business year. They are intended for use in the operations of the business and not held for sale, 20, 36

Fixed costs: tend to remain relatively constant with changes in output or sales, 76

Flow of costs: method or assumption as to how costs are charged against revenue, e.g. fifo, lifo, 32

FOB: free on board. FOB shipping point–title passes at the time delivery is made to a common carrier and goods belong to the purchaser while in transit. FOB destination–title passes when the goods reach their destination.

Footing: adding a column of figures.

Funds: commonly refers to working capital, the excess of current assets over current liabilities, 84

Funds statement: a financial statement that presents a review of financial activities that have resulted in changes in the current position. It reports the results for a given period of time, 20, 84

General journal: a book of original entry for recording transactions which cannot be recorded in the specialized journals, 16

Going concern assumption: a basic assumption that the entity will continue in existence for an indefinite period, 92

Goodwill: an intangible asset representing the cost of a purchased business in excess of the net fair market value of its assets, 42

Gross profit method: a method of estimating inventory by subtracting an estimated gross profit from actual sales, 34

Gross profit on sales: excess of net sales over the cost of goods sold, 22

Home office: main unit as distinguished from the branch(es), 72

Horizontal analysis: various measurements of changes in corresponding items in successive financial statements, 88

Income statement: financial statement which summarizes the revenue and expenses of an enterprise for a given period of time, 2, 4, 20, 22, 88

Indirect labor: that portion of the factory labor cost which cannot be identified with a special manufacturing job or process. It is considered part of factory overhead, 76

Individual proprietorship: a business enterprise owned by a single individual in which almost no preliminary legal requisites exist, 1

Installment method: a method of recognizing income as the sales proceeds are received in cash, 92

Intangible assets: assets having no physical characteristics, but which give to the business entity certain legal rights or competitive advantages. Examples are: copyrights, patents, franchises, trade marks, leaseholds and goodwill, 41

Interest, computation: principal x interest rate x time, 30

Internal control: that part of the system which relates to the plans and procedures established to: (1) safeguard the company's assets; (2) achieve accurate accounting data; (3) encourage efficient operation; and (4) measure adherence to corporate policies, 24

Inventory: merchandise held for sale in the normal course of business and supplies consumed in producing goods or services. In a manufacturing company, inventories consist of raw materials, work-in-process and finished goods, 32

Inventory turnover: computed by dividing the cost of goods sold by the average inventory, 90

Investments: property purchased to yield an income. Examples are: stocks or bonds of a domestic corporation, U.S. government securities, municipal bonds, mortgages, and long-term notes, 26

Issued stock: shares which at one time have been sold to the public. Stock reacquired by the corporation remains "issued stock," 56

Job order cost system: a cost system in which costs are accumulated for each specific job or lot manufactured, 80

Journal: the chronological record of all accounting events and the record of all pertinent information about a transaction, 6, 12

Last In-First Out: assumption as to the flow of costs in which the most recent costs are charged against revenue. The year end inventory consists of items valued at their earliest costs, 34

Ledger: total of all accounts. Ledgers are further categorized as general and subsidiary, 4

Liabilities: debts of the business, including accounts payable, notes payable, mortgages payable, and taxes payable, 64

Limited liability: an attribute of corporate ownership, limiting a stockholder's potential loss to the amount of his investment, 1, 52

Liquidation value: the amount that each share of capital stock will receive if the entity were to discontinue business and sell off all its assets, 62

Long-term liabilities: liabilities that do not satisfy the requirements for current classification. They include such items as mortgages payable and bonds payable, 22, 64

Lower of cost or market rule: basic accounting principle in the valuation of inventory. Provides for immediate recognition of loss resulting from decline in market value of inventory, 34, 92

Manufacturing costs: the raw materials, direct labor, and factory overhead costs entering into the manufacturing process, 76

Manufacturing expense: *see* Factory Overhead

Marketable securities: investments classified as current assets. They must be readily marketable and there must be an intention on the part of management to convert the investments to satisfy the cash demands of the normal operating cycle.

Market value: the price at which an item of value can be currently purchased or sold, 62

Matching concept: accounting principle of charging costs against their related revenues, 8

Materiality: relative importance must be considered as to treatment of an item and disclosure in the financial statements. Size of the amount should be considered in relation to such factors as net income and total assets, 92

Merchandise inventory: *see* Inventory.

Mortgage bonds: a certificate of indebtedness secured by a lien on real or personal property, 66

Natural resources: assets subject to depletion, such as mines, oil wells, and timber.

Net income: excess of revenues earned over expenses incurred, 22

Net worth: the capital in a corporation, consisting of capital stock, paid-in capital, and retained earnings, 60

No par value stock: shares not given a designated par or face, 52

Non-participating preferred stock: preferred stock limited in its share of corporate earnings to a fixed rate, 54

Note: written promise to pay a certain sum of money at a fixed or determinable time.

Notes payable: claims by creditors of the company, evidenced by a promissory note.

Notes receivable: claims against debtors of the company evidenced by a promissory note, 30

Notes receivable discounted: notes receivable that have been discounted at the payee's bank. The payee is contingently liable on the note, 30, 66

Notes receivable dishonored: a note which has been defaulted by the maker at maturity, 30

Objectivity: many areas in accounting are judgmental in nature. The accountant obtains objective evidence upon which to base his decision, 92

Other assets: those assets that cannot be classified as either current or fixed and include such items as long-term receivables, deferred charges, and land held for investment purposes.

Outstanding checks: checks issued by the company, not clearing the bank at the end of the month.

Outstanding stock: issued shares in the hands of the stockholders, 56

Over-applied overhead: the result of charging overhead to the jobs or departments in excess of the actual costs, 82

Overhead: *see* Factory Overhead

Owner's equity: *see* Capital

Paid-in capital in excess of par value: *see* Premium on Capital Stock, 1, 60

Parent corporation: company holding a majority of the voting shares of a second corporation, called a subsidiary, 84, 86

Participating preferred stock: preferred stock that entitles shareholders to receive dividends in excess of the fixed dividend rate, 54

Partner, admission: acquisition by an individual of a partnership interest by purchase or investment, 48

Partner's drawing: the amount of partnership assets withdrawn by a partner during the year for his personal use, 44

Partnership: a business enterprise conducted by two or more persons in which a written or oral agreement exists between the parties, 1, 44

Partner's investment: represents the partner's contribution to the partnership, 44

Partner withdrawal: upon leaving the partnership a partner may receive cash or other assets from either the remaining partner(s) or from the partnership, 50

Par value stock: share of stock that has been given an arbitrary face value which usually is nominal in relationship to the actual fair market value of the shares, 52

Percentage of contract completion: accounting method whereby revenue is recognized over the period of the contract based upon the percentage of completion of the project, 94

Period costs: those costs which should be immediately charged to revenues without passing through the inventory accounts, 76

Periodic inventory system: a method of determining inventory quantities based solely on a physical count of the merchandise taken at the end of the accounting period, 32

Perpetual inventory system: a method of determining inventory quantities based on detailed records maintained for each item of inventory. Accuracy of records is verified by annual physical count, 32, 80

Petty cash fund: special cash fund for handling small disbursements. Fund is replenished by transfer from regular cash account, 24-26

Plant assets: *see* Fixed Assets.

Point of sale: revenue realized at the time title passes, 92

Posting: the process whereby the transactions recorded in the journals are entered in the ledger, 6

Post-closing trial balance: general ledger trial balance taken after the closing entries have been recorded.

Predetermined factory overhead rate: the rate used in applying overhead to a job or department.

Pre-emptive right: the right of a shareholder to maintain his proportional ownership in a corporation by purchasing a pro rata number of shares of any additional issuances of stock, 52, 58

Preference as to assets: the right inherent in certain preferred stock which entitles the holders to liquidating distributions before any payments are made to common shareholders, 54

Preferred stock: class of stock which is entitled to share in the corporation's earnings at a fixed rate prior to payments to common shareholders, 52, 54

Premium on capital stock: the difference between the amount received on the issuance of capital stock and the par or stated value of the shares, 56

Prepaid expenses: unexpended portion of an expense already paid. Classified as a current asset.

Process cost system: a cost accounting system in which average unit costs are determined for an accounting period. Can be utilized only when a homogeneous product is produced, 80, 82

Product costs: those costs associated with the manufacture of the product, 76

Profit and loss summary: *see* Revenue and Expense Summary.

Progressive tax: a tax in which the tax rate increases as the taxable base increases, 96

Purchase discount: cash discounts taken by the purchaser and reflected on his books.

Purchase journal: a book of original entry used to record transactions with the suppliers of goods and services to the business enterprise. The purchase invoice is the accounting document that provides the source for entry, 12, 14, 68

Quick ratio: *see* Acid Test Ratio.

Raw materials: goods that enter into and become part of the manufactured article, 76

Reciprocal account concept: accounts which are in agreement but have opposite balances (i.e., one a debit, one a credit), 72

Redemption value: price to be paid by the issuing corporation when repurchasing a preferred stock or bond issue. The amount is set slightly above the par or face value, 62

Registered bond: a type of bond in which interest and principal payments are made only to the individual indicated as owner on the corporate records, 66

Retail inventory method: a method of determining inventory value used in the retail trade. A book inventory is arrived at by applying the ratio prevailing between cost and sales prices to the sales for the period, 34

Retained earnings: undistributed profits of the corporation, 1, 60

Retained earnings statement: a financial statement which reports changes in the retained earnings account for a given period of time, 60

Revenue and expense summary: the account to which all income and expense accounts are closed at the end of an accounting period.

Revenue expenditure: those items which are properly charged as an expense against revenues. Contrasted with capital expenditure, 40

Revenues: represent the gross increment attributable to business activity. Sources of revenue include sales of merchandise for cash or credit, fees for services rendered and dividend and interest income, 2, 92

Reversing entries: certain adjusting entries affect the recording of otherwise normal transactions in the following accounting period. To eliminate such a problem in the new period the original adjustment is reversed, i.e. the debits become the credits and the credits become debits, 10

Sales: gross charge for merchandise, reduced by returns, allowances and discounts, 22

Sales discount: cash discounts taken by seller and reflected on his books.

Sales journal: a book of original entry used to record sale of goods on open account. Source for entering transactions is the sales invoice, 12

Selling, general and administrative expenses: items incurred directly by the normal merchandising operations of the business. In a manufacturing company expense items not classified in cost of goods sold or other expense.

Semi-variable costs: costs which vary to some degree with activity changes, 76

Serial bonds: several maturity dates of a particular bond issue, 66

Shares of stock: units of ownership in the corporation, 56

Sinking fund bonds: bond issues which require the creation of a special fund to accumulate the money necessary to retire the bonds at maturity, 66

Source and application of funds statement: *see* Funds Statement.

Sources of funds: any transaction that increases the working capital of an enterprise, 84

Specialized journal: any book of original entry in which all items of a similar nature are recorded. Specialized journals include sales, purchase, cash receipts, and cash disbursements, 12

Specific identification: inventory method in which the actual cost of the specific item is used.

Stability of the monetary unit assumption: for accounting purposes, a 1939 dollar is identical with a current dollar. Price-level changes are ignored, 92

Standard costs: scientifically predetermined estimates, 82

Stated value stock: stock which has no face value but which is assigned a value by the board of directors. This stated value bears no relationship to either fair market value or book value, 52

Stock: *see* Shares of Stock, Common Stock, Preferred Stock, and Capital Stock.

Stock dividend: a dividend paid in additional shares of common stock of the corporation. Retained earnings are charged for the fair market value of the shares issued, 60, 62

Stock split-up: reduction of the par or stated value of a corporation's common stock and the issuance of a proportionate number of additional shares, 62

Stockholders' equity: *see* Net Worth.

Subscriptions to the capital stock: before the actual receipt of cash or other assets from the future stockholders they often agree to subscribe to the shares. The subscription agreement is binding and therefore an asset exists on the corporation's books, 58

Subsidiary corporation: a company that is controlled by another corporation, called its parent, which owns a majority of its voting shares, 84, 86

Subsidiary ledger: where a business has a large number of accounts of the same type it is customary to segregate these into a separate ledger. Common subsidiary ledgers are accounts receivable, accounts payable and fixed assets, 12, 14, 41

Term bonds: all the bonds of an issue mature at the same time, 66

Transaction: an accounting or business transaction is the occurrence of an event or a condition that must be recorded.

Treasury stock: shares once issued by the corporation which have subsequently been reacquired, 56, 58

Trial balance: listing of all the account balances in a ledger as of a given date. The general ledger trial balance is used to establish the equality of debits and credits that have been posted, 6

Uncollectible accounts: accounts receivable which have proved to be uncollectible.

Under-applied overhead: The result of charging overhead to jobs or departments at less than the actual costs, 82

Underwriting costs: costs or fees paid by the corporation in marketing its securities. The issuing corporation enters in its books only the net amount received, 56

Unissued stock: those which have never been sold by the corporation, 56

Variable costs: directly correlated to activity, 76

Variances: differences between actual and standard costs, 82

Vertical analysis: measures the relationships among the items in a single set of financial statements, 88

Voucher: document prepared by the purchaser of goods or services on which is recorded all of the pertinent data relating to the liability, 68

Voucher register: a book of original entry in which all vouchers are entered. Used as a replacement for the accounts payable journal and the accounts payable subsidiary ledger, 68

Voucher system: an accounting method of exercising control over the disbursement of cash. Voucher, voucher register, check register and files of paid and unpaid vouchers are used, 68, 70

Weighted Average: inventory method in which costs are charged against revenues on the basis of a computed average. Weighted averages are determined by dividing the total costs incurred in acquiring the units available for sale by the total number of units, 34

Work-in-process: partially completed goods in the process of production, 80

Working capital: the excess of current assets over current liabilities, 20, 84, 88, 90

Work sheet: a form used to assist in the preparation of formal financial statements. The sets of money columns include trial balance, adjustments, income statement and balance sheet, 8